UNCONDITIONAL

Raymie Andrews

Copyright © 2021 by Raymie Andrews

All rights reserved. No part of this publication may be reproduced, distributed, or transmitted in any form or by any means, including photocopying, recording, or other electronic or mechanical methods, without the prior written permission of the publisher, except in the case brief quotations embodied in critical reviews and other noncommercial uses permitted by copyright law.

ISBN: 978-1-63945-096-1 (Paperback)

The views expressed in this book are solely those of the author and do not necessarily reflect the views of the publisher, and the publisher hereby disclaims any responsibility for them.

Writers' Branding
1800-608-6550
www.writersbranding.com
orders@writersbranding.com

Contents

DEDICATION v

Chapter 1   SCOTT AND FRIENDS 1
Chapter 2   A MOTHER'S PRAYER 7
Chapter 3   FORDS, COWS, AND GOD'S CALL 15
Chapter 4   A MAJOR DREAM COMES TRUE 23
Chapter 5   EXPECT THE UNEXPECTED FROM GOD 33
Chapter 6   THE FIGHT BETWEEN THE BOY AND THE MAN 41
Chapter 7   IT'S ABOUT PEOPLE 51
Chapter 8   THE LOVE OF MY LIFE 59
Chapter 9   BACK TO ROME 65
Chapter 10 A MINISTRY OF A DIFFERENT KIND 77
Chapter 11 FACING DOWN RACISM 83
Chapter 12 HALL COUNTY: THE POPLAR SPRINGS YEARS 93
Chapter 13 HALL COUNTY: THE FLOWERY BRANCH YEARS 105
Chapter 14 A KID NAMED TRENT 123
Chapter 15 STUDENTS AND MISSIONS 131
Chapter 16 SOME THINGS I KNOW 145
Chapter 17 INTO THE FUTURE 155
Chapter 18 FINGERPRINTS 165

DEDICATION

On Monday, October 15, 2007, a simple yet profound man entered into heaven. His name was Charles William Wiley, my father. It is the way he lived his life that taught me the meaning of unconditional love.

Out of his faith he quietly helped widows, black people, poor people, alcoholics, and anyone who needed him. He did it in the spirit of Jesus in a day when it was not fashionable in South Georgia for white people and black people to be close friends.

Because of his simple faith, the way he set the bar high for Christ-like living, and because he loved people, ALL people, unconditionally, I dedicate this book to his life and the legacy he has left behind for me, my mother, and my sister to follow. May we all learn to love more, and to love unconditionally.

CHAPTER ONE

SCOTT AND FRIENDS

I walked into the room and there they were. They were seated on benches, surrounded by the cold metal of lockers and the smell of a locker room. All eyes were fixed on me. These 8th graders, 13 and 14 years old, knew they were seeing me potentially for the last time. These young men for some reason had really come to love me. My love for them had become indescribable.

There was Caleb, the quarterback, a tall, blonde, blue eyed package of 13 year old coolness under fire. Travis sat there quietly looking down. Brian was slumped over in his pads and looking up at me. Nick sat tall and looked at me with pools of water forming at the edges of his blue eyes. Marquis was there with his usual quiet calm. I looked at him and for a moment it seemed as if I knew there were great athletic things in store for him in the future. Dylan was dressed out in his pads, his helmet resting on his lap. J.D.'s brown eyes were fixed hard on me. I loved J.D. more then he knew. When you have been honored to bring a young teen to faith, you love them. They become very special trophies. Daniel, the center, was his usual stoic self, not showing much emotion ever. This kid was a monster for his age, and an excellent football player. His physical size was also indicative of the size of his heart. Big-eyed and dimpled, he had moved from the grass-stained kid on the hill on Friday nights to a friend who had set his sights on winning a game for a 51 year old man who had shown him some Christian love and attention.

And there was Scott. He was not "wired" the same as the other boys. Scott's mind was creative, funny, and random at times, with a sense of humor that was "out there" and even a bit sick in a healthy teenaged way. I knew that underneath the weirdness was a young man who was sensitive, kind, intelligent, and crying out for validation by his peers and the adults in his life. If he and I were ever in the same room, he was right there by my side. But today, he had his game face on . . . serious, focused, and sad.

As the coach stood by my side, I spoke briefly to them. I do not remember what I said. My emotions were running deep. This was it. I asked them if they would not be offended to please join me in prayer. Those who did not want to were free to not participate. They all bowed. At that moment, Baptists, Methodists, Charismatic, Catholics, Muslims, and boys who really were not sure what they believed had all come together.

It was game day Thursday. It was the final game of these boys' Middle School experience. They would never play another football game for West Hall Middle School. The "amen" was said. I waved, told them I loved them, and exited the locker room. As I walked out the door, through the gate and began the short journey across the football field, the hard drive that is my mind began to play back files of memories saved from five years of loving West Hall Middle School. The past three years, when these boys were only 6th graders, small, voices often not even squeaking yet from the onslaught of puberty, until now when they are tall, deep-voiced 8th grade young men, had been especially wonderful. Somehow I had bonded with these boys in the three years I had been the unofficial chaplain of the school.

Now, it had all come down to this. I was joining the staff of a church an hour away in another county on the other side of Atlanta. No longer would I visit that school every Wednesday during the school year. My leadership and help with 1st Priority, the Christian club there, had come to an end. I would not be there for basketball games, soccer games, football games, band concerts, sitting across a lunchroom table listening to a problem or encouraging a kid whose mom was all he had and was struggling with cancer. The days were coming to an end when I would sit with "The Mob" and laugh at jokes and drink a pack of hot sauce without flinching or crying. I would no longer mediate the girl cat fights they would come to me about.

As I climbed the steps to the top of the stadium I remembered all those Friday nights of standing in groups of students talking to them, walking the top of the stadium and hearing my name called, watching the middle school boys roll down the hill on the visitor's side trying to impress the girls. I remembered standing behind the band as they played their hearts out for the High School team on Friday nights and encouraging them.

I remembered one night clearly. I was walking past the concession area when Trent came running up to me with a look of panic on his face, shoved his cell phone to my ear as he said, "Listen to this." He hit the message button. "Trent, Come home as soon as you get this. Your grandmother has been taken to the hospital," I heard his mother say in her New York brogue.

"Can I take you home, Trent?"

He looked at me and uttered a helpless "yes."

"Who did you come to the game with?"

"Jody."

"Find Jody and tell him that I am taking you home and tell him what is going on." He found Jody and returned to me. Just as we were walking out of the stadium, way before half-time, Trent's father arrived at the gate to find him. Thanking me for the help, Trent and his dad were on their way.

Three years. Time, money, love, praying, and sacrifice had all come down to this. A sunny Thursday afternoon, just slightly cool, after school, an 8th grade football team, and for a moment it was just me and the stadium, and my thoughts. Slowly the stadium began to fill. Students found me one-by-one, and we all sat together. Eric and Mike knew this was the end. So did Michael. Justin was there too. It was clear that without ever discussing it, we had all decided that this afternoon was going to be fun. It was going to be a party. We would enjoy being together one more time. We would celebrate the love and friendship we all enjoyed even after the final buzzer went off announcing the end of the game.

The cheerleaders were cranking it up. North Hall Middle School was the opponent, and a formidable foe. With disciplined kids on the team and excellent coaching they were at the top of the heap in the county. They took the field confidently. The West Hall cheerleaders put up the banner they had worked on with love and devotion to the team and the school only to have it ripped apart as "my boys" came roaring and growling and applauding through the paper art work. I saw glimpses of eyes through helmets looking at the stands to spot where I was. Once spotted, I could see the corners of their eyes turn up in a smile.

And the game was on! West Hall scored first. Caleb seemed very much in command on that first drive. The entire team looked really good marching toward the goal line. But North Hall tied the game up at halftime. The score was 8-8. In the third quarter North Hall pulled ahead on a touchdown. Missing the two point conversion, the score then became 14-8. West Hall seemed to lose momentum. North Hall threatened to score again.

Then I saw a miracle. North Hall fumbled and West Hall came up with the ball! With just a minute and a half left in the game West Hall came alive. Marquis ran a reverse for yardage. Then it happened.

Caleb launched the ball high toward the end zone to Travis, who pulled the ball in to his chest tightly. There was no stopping him. He scored, running into the end zone to tie the game. The whole team kept glancing up into the stands where I had become maniacal. On the two-point conversion Marquis found the hole and ran it in. West Hall now had the lead.

But the miracles did not stop there. There was enough time on the clock for North Hall to run at least two plays and potentially score and win. North Hall's quarterback reared back to throw long downfield to his receiver. Out of nowhere, Marquis was there, intercepted the ball, taking it back from North Hall. The West Hall team took a knee on the play and ran out the clock as I walked onto the field. I watched them with tears in my eyes as they celebrated on the field, jumping up and down, slapping one another on the back, hugging, and congratulating one another. Then, one-by- one, they came. "That was for you," they said. Together we celebrated, and then knelt on the field as Coach Newfall talked to the boys who had become very much young men. Then he asked me to pray . . . again. After we prayed the celebration continued. Brian introduced me to his mother, who took a picture of Brian and me together on the field. I chatted with the players as they came by. I talked with the school resource officer. Then the time came.

I walked with the team up to the field house and thanked them outside the door. As I walked to the car it seemed I was having one of those movie moments where the camera suddenly shifts into slow motion and everything becomes quiet. In the car, CD player off, I wept hard all the way home.

That day is burned into my memory forever. God spoke to me deeply that day. Through a group of sweaty, smelly, 8th grade jocks God confirmed what I already knew and had always sought to practice in ministering to students, but had never really experienced so fully. When you love people without condition, they will "get it" and when they "get it" they will love you back in some startling and unexpected ways.

Scott Eichler and his friends, Nick Osborne, Travis Clements, Josh Preston, Caleb Stewart, Daniel Drummond, Ryan Bozarth, Brian Ernst, Cale Collins, J.D. Wolfe, Jae Neal, Marquis Stephens, and Benny Braza, Matt Boone, and Dylan Bartlette were the voice of God to me that fall day on Thursday, September 30, 2004.

The purpose of this book is not to say that when you give unconditional love to kids that you should expect something in return. It often does not happen that way, nor should a student pastor's motive be to have a football game dedicated to them and won for them. If that happens it is an awesome thing, but that can never be our motive, to get honor and glory for ourselves. Our ministries are to be all about God. What we do as student pastors must be done as offerings pleasing to God so that He gets the glory. It is up to God and God alone what rewards He bestows on us this side of eternity.

This book is written to hopefully inspire student pastors, young and old, to persevere, to stay pure, to unconditionally love students, ALL students. When I walk into a High School or a Middle School, or when I am at an athletic event or concert at a school I am struck with the diversity of students. Some look pretty normal by our adult standards of "normal." Then there are those who are so dark, dressed in black, paled-out make up and black lipstick with fingernails dark as coal. There is the emo boy with the haircut and the glasses and the girl pants, t-shirt, and Converse shoes. Look around further and there are the kids who have so many pieces of metal in their faces and other parts of their anatomy that they would be no fun to carry through an airport on a mission trip. There are the "redneck" good old boys with the tight jeans and cowboy hats. There is the prep girl dressed to the teeth with an attitude to match. Among those students are those struggling with gay and lesbian issues, black, white, Asian, Middle Eastern, Hispanic, Mexican, and the list can go on and on.

Student pastors have come to a place in history where student ministry is both fun, more exciting than ever, but also more challenging than ever. The stakes are higher in the lives of our students. It seems that the forces of darkness have raised the bar on us saying to us, "Okay! Love THIS unconditionally." And God watches us to see if we will rise to the challenge. We are in a life and death fight for the lives of our students. I have stayed in the battle for 32 years. I have learned some things along the way, sometimes through laughter and sometimes through a broken heart. If a student pastor or anyone reading this finds some nugget of wisdom or encouragement to stay in the fight, my years of student ministry will not have been in vain. I understand that I am at a time in my life now when I can pass along to the next generation of student pastors the things I know that are true. I have a responsibility now not only to students I encounter, but to other younger youth pastors. My prayer is that God will send some kids like Scott, Travis, Lori, Melissa, Trent, Josh, and others that you may meet in this book into your life. For as I have sought to bless the lives of kids like these, they have consistently blessed me back.

However, there are some kids I have loved unconditionally and as far as I can determine, they could not have cared any less, and have never responded to the love of God I sought to plant into their lives. I will never know until heaven if they "got it." I have hope that they did.

So, allow me to walk you through my life, my ministry from the early rumblings of God's call on my life, how I dropped the ball at times in my early ministry, and what I have learned. Along the way, I want to introduce to you some of my friends. Already you have met that 8th grade football team. There are other students, some who are married with children now, that I want you to meet. Their stories will perhaps encourage you. Some of the decisions they have made for their lives will disappoint you. Even in that, my prayer is that their stories will cause you to pray more, love harder, and minister fearlessly to the toughest kid God will put in your path.

We are called to love unconditionally. That is not in our nature. It is something I had to learn to practice as a believer. Let's start the journey now. It begins with a mother in 1953 in Sycamore, Georgia.

CHAPTER TWO

A MOTHER'S PRAYER

On September 19, 1953, Charles and Willene Wiley became the parents of a son . . . me. Mother was barely 20 and my dad was in business and trying to go to night school. It had to be a challenge for them once I was born. I have some memories of the garage apartment we lived in. It was upstairs over the garage on the property with a great aunt and uncle.

I remember it as dark, but clean and comfortable. There was an old green radio in the apartment with some kind of cat on top of it. It was a small but nice apartment for a young couple just beginning life together. My arrival made it all the more interesting for them I am sure.

Does anyone remember bassinettes? Do they still use them? It's a bed for a baby. It looks like a basket with legs and maybe a hood over the top. That is where I slept in that apartment. I am certain that my mother, like all mothers, would come and stand by the bassinette and just watch her baby sleep. I wonder what goes through a mother's mind when they look at their children sleeping sometimes. They must dream of what they would have their sons and daughters become. In their minds they plan weddings, wonder about the spiritual welfare of that child, how they will provide for them all the necessities of life, how they will raise that child so they grow up strong and well-adjusted and successful. I'm sure they talk to God often about that sleeping child.

As I began to grow, they understood that the apartment was going to be too small, especially since my sister arrived right after my third birthday. So, dad began to build a house on family property, a house of our own. I remember the day he took me to the building site. He stood me in a spot on the sub flooring and told me the very spot I was standing on would be my very own bedroom. I could not believe it. All that was there were wood and some studs where the walls were beginning to come up. I remember feeling that dad was looking out for me. He was building me "my place."

We moved in. I had "my place" and my sister had hers. Mom and dad had their room. It was as not long before a color TV appeared in our home to take the place of the old black and white, and the radio gave way to the stereo console in the living room that filled the home with music of all kinds. It was our home. I grew up there. My 12th and 13th years were rebellious and stormy at times. Things were happening in that home despite my rebellious nature that were God's hand moving and answering a prayer.

At the age of 9 I began my personal journey of faith in that home. Something was going on deep in my little boy soul that was scaring me to death. It all came together as we rode home in the black Ford car from revival. I held it in as long as I could. As I stepped out of the car, I burst out crying hard. Mom was giving me this look and asked, "What in the world is wrong with you?" Dad was standing on the other side of the car listening as I blurted it out. "I don't want to go to Hell!"

The next day, Pastor Clint Brown and the revival evangelist arrived at our door early in the afternoon. Preacher Brown was a huge man. To a young boy he was Goliath. He had come to share Jesus with me. I sat in his lap as he showed me in the Bible how much God loves me and how Jesus came to die for me to take away my sin. It was pretty clear I did not have to go to Hell. That day in the corner of that den in that house dad built this nine year old knelt and asked Jesus to be Lord of his life.

Sycamore Baptist Church is one of two churches in Turner County, Georgia that God used to answer a prayer. My bent was becoming more and more toward music and singing. I was not going to be a star athlete. That church invested in me. They made sure that every year I was eligible that I attended the Georgia Baptist Youth Music Camp. It was there one summer that God spoke to me again.

12 year olds are strange people. They are not little boys anymore really, but not full-grown men either. Girls become an issue. The world begins to open up to them. Strange things start going on with their bodies. It is as if aliens come and possess them. The summer of my twelfth year I was at music camp. All week long the flirting had gone on. Her name was Sylvia. She had the prettiest red hair and the nicest southern accent I had ever heard. I am sure from her smile, too, that there must have been 100 teeth in there! We hit it off as good friends. The Sunday worship service came

around. We all went to the chapel for the service. We sang. It sounded almost angelic, a taste of music in heaven, because we all were musical that were there. Then some man preached that they called the camp pastor. I do not remember his name. I have no clue what he preached about. I was glad to be sitting next to Sylvia in that service. All was right with the world . . . until the altar call was given. Suddenly, God was speaking to me clearly.

"Frankie, give me your talents."

"God. I am not going down there and surrender anything to you. What if you make me a missionary to Africa and I wind up with cannibals as their main course!?"

Remember that rebellious nature I spoke of earlier? It came out to play. Inside my soul I was miserable. God was not getting my talents. I was not so sure I liked preachers and music people either. I knew they were Godly people, but something about them just did not appeal to me. I did not want to be one of them. "Wherever He Leads, I'll Go" was the song being sung. I grabbed the pew and held on for dear life.

Dr. Paul McCommon was the state music man for Georgia Baptists at the time. He reminded me of a Weeble. He was short, rounded, with a bald head, and he sort of wobbled as he directed music. He was down front receiving people who came forward at that service. God was pounding on me big time by now.

"God, If I go down there I will have to push past Sylvia and I might step on her or "Bump her because, God, you know how clumsy I am!"

That was the truth. I was clumsy. Sylvia then stepped out and went to the front! It was a clear shot to the aisle. What was to stop me now? The next thing I remember is telling Dr. Paul that I did not really know what God wanted me to do but he could have my talents. There in that chapel in Toccoa, Georgia God won. I gave Him my music. I had no idea what a ferocious battle would ensue because of that commitment.

I returned from camp to form a rock band. Sure, God could have my talents, but it is so cool playing in a rock band. My cousin Chris played bass, Dale Wiggins played the keyboard, David Royal was our lead guitarist, Steve Hobby played the drums, and I was the lead vocalist and rhythm guitar player. We played tons of dances. We got lots of female attention. We even won the local Battle of the Bands, only to go on to the regional and be soundly defeated. We did not care. We were cool. We were local rock stars. Everyone at school knew about us. But, in my heart something was not right. I had given my talents to God, but was not using them for him. I was around things that were dangerous and ungodly because of this. Then I had to make a decision.

One night after a dance at the American Legion Home, the phone rang. It was David. He was really upbeat and excited. "Dude, great news."

"Oh, really? What's going on? "I hired us a manager."

"Wow! That is awesome. Who did you get?" "Tommy"

When he said the guy's name I nearly dropped the phone and I got this really sick feeling in my stomach. Our new manager was also the biggest drug dealer in town. I knew it for a fact. When you are sixteen in a small town, you know everyone's business at the High School. Tommy was dangerous. I had seen him hanging out at the dance that night listening to us, and probably making a few bucks, too. Then I got mad.

"Do you know who that guy is?" I asked.

"He can really make some things happen for us."

"David, he's the biggest drug dealer in town. Sure he can open doors but at what price?"

"Well, he's going to be our manager."

"Okay. If Tommy is going to be the manager he will have to manage the band without me.

Once again, God was beginning to move and arrange circumstances in answer to a prayer.

It was not long after that incident that I was asked to be the pianist for the Youth Revival coming up at Bethel Baptist Church. I had found that Bethel was better equipped to minister to a kid like me and with my parents' blessing I had become a member there. It was the final night of revival. Ted Moody was preaching. Corky Goe was the music leader. The invitation hymn was "Just as I Am." I sat at the piano knowing how I was! I was a 16 year old who had given his talents to God four years ago, then taken them back to use for his own glorification. God was reminding me of that moment in Toccoa. I began to weep. Tears started splashing down on my hands and all over the keyboard of the piano. I could barely see the music in front of me. And again, that rebellious nature stepped forward. "Frankie, if you go down to the altar the music will stop. Corky won't have an accompanist and will be flapping his arms up there trying to sing with no music and you will have made him look really stupid. You stay and play."

There was a tap on my right shoulder. My first thought was that I had become so stubborn that God had to get physical with me now. As I turned to look, Mrs. Helen Jordan, the organist at a Methodist church and piano teacher in town, leaned over to me and whispered sweetly, "Would you like me to play so you can do down to the altar?" We swapped hands off the keyboard. Corky's reputation was saved. I made things right again with the Father. He now had me, unconditionally, all in answer to a prayer.

During my Senior year I was determined to live for God. I was able to see many of my friends come to faith. I led one friend to Jesus who turned around and came to Bethel and stole my girlfriend! I helped start the first Bible club at Turner County High School. I kept my Bible on top of my books at school, and read it. Amazingly, some of my friends would pick it up before class and read in it. I finished High School and had wondered what I would do about college. The family did not have a lot of money. God always met our needs, but college was expensive. Where would I go? How would I afford it? God was already working it out because of a prayer.

One afternoon I entered the house in the usual way after school, the back door under the carport. As I entered I noticed a stack of mail on the bar that was our dining table and divided the den from the kitchen. I thumbed through the stack. There was actually something for me in that stack of mail. It was from Brewton-Parker Junior College music department. I curiously opened the letter. What I read brought me to my knees alone there in the den. Hildegard Stanley was the Chairperson of the Music Department at Brewton-Parker College. She was also one of the staffers at Georgia Baptist Youth Music Camp. The letter was offering me full scholarship to come to Brewton-Parker. I could receive scholarships for vocals, guitar, keyboard, singing in the chorus, if I was a ministerial student, if my grades were good, and on the list went. I could not believe my eyes. I knelt by the couch there and gave God a big "Thank You" for answering my prayers. I was college-bound with every penny paid. However, it was not just my prayers for God to show me how to go to college. It was in answer to another prayer.

I attended Brewton-Parker Junior College, and then the door opened for me to finish my Bachelor's degree in Church Music at Shorter College, perhaps the best and toughest music school in the state of Georgia. Between college and seminary I spent three years at a church in Rome, Georgia, and then attended The Southern Baptist Theological Seminary in Louisville, Kentucky, where I received a double Master of Divinity in Religious Education of Youth degree. That was a tough three years. Academically it stretched me to the limits. My belief system was challenged at every turn. My ethics and morality were shaken out, broken, and reformed. God was polishing me up because the time was approaching when I would launch out full-time ministering to students and using my musical skills as a tool to reach them. It is funny what you don't know when you are twelve. All I knew was that God wanted my talents and He could have them. I thought I would just be a Minister of Music somewhere flapping my arms on Sunday trying to hold all the singers and musicians together. Worship leaders are in a prime position to do something that can be difficult in a Baptist Church. They actually get the whole church agreeing together and in harmony, if only for an hour. I had no clue that God was up to something beyond acting out each Sunday the old gospel hymn "I'll Fly Away." It all was happening because of a prayer.

There was something that my mother had not told me. At least she pondered it in her heart just like Mary I guess, until one special day. I was home visiting my parents. I love doing that to this day. I am not sure exactly when in the flow of my life she told me this. It could have been once while I was home from seminary, or home on holiday early in my ministry right after seminary. We were talking about church and ministry and how God was using me. I remember being content now that my life was headed down the road of ministry with no turning back. I had expressed that to her. She looked at me in her own special way and said, "I want to tell you something. There was a day when you were a baby when I was standing by your crib looking at you while you slept. I realized that I could not raise you. I prayed and asked God to help me and your daddy raise you, and I also gave you up to God that day for Him to do with you whatever He wanted to do. God has answered that prayer."

Sons of Godly mothers, rejoice! They are praying for you. Even my grandmother Wiley was in on the praying! Every major meeting with God that has happened in my life is a direct result of that one prayer of a young mother who felt unqualified to raise me and cried out to God for help, surrendering me to His will. My mother's unconditional love for me and her prayers has made all the difference in my life to this very day. Let me add that I have had a Godly daddy too, who loved me and has prayed for me, and agonized over me in ways I will never know. But, that one prayer from my mother I believe made all the difference. I was not an easy child to rear. There is stubbornness, rebellion, a strong-willed temperament, a personality prone to melancholy at times, and even a false sense of invulnerability in me. The Bible is true. Rebelliousness is bound in the heart of a child, but the rod of correction will drive it far from them. Discipline and a mother's prayers are a powerful combination. I am forever grateful for that one prayer prayed over me in my infancy. It follows me and shapes me to this day. Thanks, mom!

CHAPTER THREE

FORDS, COWS, AND GOD'S CALL

The Minister of Music. The "kwar" director. That's how they say it in Georgia. Once I entered the hallowed halls of Brewton-Parker College I became a "ministerial student." I was one of those preacher boys on campus headed for work in a church. "Preacher Boy." I hated that title. I have always disliked "titles" but this one really worked on my psyche. But that's what I was to that campus, like it or not, a preacher boy. I wasn't even going to preach. I had given God my music. It stopped there.

I began to be asked to speak at BSU worship in that little white chapel, only to turn them down. Dr. Quattlebaum, one of the college professors there asked me to come to his little country church and lead their music on Sundays. I did that with fear and trembling. It was there that I should have known God was up to something broader than the choir director. I first heard these words there: "Our youth don't have anyone to spend time with them. You are young. Would you mind doing some things with our youth?"

First, since when does being young qualify one to minister to teenagers? I now believe that student pastors should probably begin their ministries with students no younger than 25 years of age. I was barely 18 when I first heard those words beckoning me to spend time with teenagers. I was still a teenager myself. I was not far enough removed from them age-wise to be effective. I had no training in that area. I was very immature. I made some terrible mistakes. I was still working through personal spiritual issues of my own. How could I possibly speak to their needs? And, I was not even sure I liked teenagers.

Teenagers . . . silly, sometimes smelly, pimple-faced pubescent people that can be really annoying . . . that was how I saw them. I reluctantly would sing and play guitar for them, and maybe do a fellowship as long as the parents were actually doing the work. To stand in front of them and do a Bible study was out of the question. I did not want to be a preacher boy. For that first year, I concentrated on the music end and "threw the youth a bone or two here and there." I was not going to preach. I did not want to preach and teach. BSU needed to leave me alone. I was on one of their evangelism teams. Bill Hardee could do the preaching. Just let me sing and lead the music. Was that not enough? The youth at church liked it when I played guitar and sang. My first year was spent in inner rebellion against God nudging me to broaden the ministry He was calling me to.

I spent that first summer after my freshman year at Ocilla Baptist Church as their summer youth director. I had lots of swimming parties, a lock-in, and an evangelistic push into the community there that summer. But what I concentrated on was the musical that church's youth choir and another choir had combined to learn and perform by summer's end. Music was what I was called to do.

The evening of the performance of "Tell It Like It Is" was tremendous. My parents were there. Ocilla Baptist Church had a balcony that went along the back and sides of the church somewhat. Even the balcony was packed out with teenagers sitting in the floor with their legs dangling through the rails. There were chairs in the aisle downstairs. The drummer, Bruce Dorminey, the guitarist, the flautist, the bassist, and the keyboardist were all in place. The performance was incredible. They played and sang their hearts out. I was in tears when it was over. I was born to do this. It felt good, like a well-worn pair of jeans on a day off. I returned to college for my sophomore year feeling like I had really found God's niche for me.

This year would be my second year traveling and performing with The Folk Four, a PR singing quartet with guitar that sang in schools and churches. I was also back in the huge college chorus that sounded like heaven when we all sang together. I was a Baron Singer, a select group of students who performed sacred and novelty pieces for various events. I was doing my thing . . . music. Forget the preaching. This was the most fun in the world for me. I was a ministerial student having the ride of my life. I had seen nothing yet. God was preparing me for some correction and a huge touch of His forgiving grace.

I had come home for the weekend. To this day, I am notorious for sleeping late when I have no urgent business to attend to on my day off or on Saturdays when I'm not involved in an event of ministry. I was sleeping in and loving it. Mom and dad were out of the house. I was alone, asleep, and safe and warm in my own bed. What more could a busy and very tired college student ask for, than one Saturday back home to do laundry and just sleep?

I had to be dreaming. I heard the phone ringing. As the persistent blare of the phone brought me to consciousness I sleepily rolled over, stared at the brown handset there by the bed, and thought words a ministerial student needs to repent of. "Hello!" On the other end of the line was Dean Knight from the college.

In a sleepy and borderline rude tone I asked, "What do you want?"

"Milan Baptist Church has called me for someone to fill their pulpit because their pastor had suddenly taken ill. I need you to go preach for that church."

My first thought was "I ain't preaching! How do I get out of this one?"

Suddenly my mind was fully awake and in a very creative mode. I remembered that Chris was my cousin. I remembered that he was also my roommate. He needed a ride back to school Sunday with me. And I had already told Lindsey that we would meet him at the I-75 exit there in town and take him with us back to campus that afternoon after church. WHEW! I had found my way out of this one!

"Dean Knight, I really can't do this. You see, Chris Brown and Lindsey Collins are depending on me to get them back to school on Sunday. If I go to that church they will have no way back to school."

"I need you to work this out."

I apologetically replied, "I cannot do it. I'm sorry." I then immediately hung up the phone.

I rolled over, and went back to sleep, thanking God I did not have to do that.

On Sunday, I got up, dressed well, and drove out to Bethel Baptist Church. I walked in the door like some conquering hero returned from battle. There were hugs and kisses and handshakes and well-wishers and conversation about school. I stood in that congregation and lifted my voice and sang to God like I was dead center in His will. All was well. I played the game and fooled them all . . . yet, not all of them; for God was there and He knew well I had once again been a rebellious and stubborn King's kid.

I returned home, ate lunch with my parents and my sister, loaded up my 1964 Ford Custom with my guitar and freshly washed clothes, and set out for Brownville to pick up Chris. Chris loaded his guitar and freshly washed clothes in. I loved that car. It was white, sleek, powerful, and had cherry red interior in great condition. Inside was a state-of-the-art system . . . an 8-track player with four speakers. Chris and I talked and motored up to the exit on I-75 and met Lindsey, who loaded his freshly washed clothes and his trumpet into the car. And there we were . . . three college students with not a care in the world roaring down Georgia roads from Sycamore to Mt. Vernon. The drive would take about 90 minutes. That is what we thought.

The sun began to set. Day turned to a blazing sky that paled into darkness as we drove. We were approaching the city limits of Milan, Georgia. It was dark. I had just turned on the headlights. The three of us were talking and laughing as college students will do. As I rounded a curve doing almost 60 miles per hour I saw movement on the highway shoulder to my right. I hit the brakes hard, yelled out, "Cows! Duck!" as my beautiful car slammed into a herd of Black Angus cattle loose from the fences and crossing the road. I took out two of them. I had tried to position the car in between the two. What resulted was horrendous. The lead cow was hit to her rear. At the same time the other cow was slammed hard in the head and front of the body. The momentum of the impact swerved the lead cow to my left around so that her head banged hard into the driver's side window. The second cow was slung around so that her rear smacked hard into the passenger side of the car. Meanwhile from the back seat, I clearly heard the passenger back there scream something about the offspring of a dog. I managed to hold the car in the road and bring it to a stop.

Another car soon approached the wreck and other cars began to gather to see the bizarre scene of one cow in one ditch, the other cow in the other ditch, three college students standing outside the car checking ourselves out for injuries, and a herd of cattle running for their lives. The front of the car was a crumpled mess, hood up! I surveyed the damage, only to discover that my white car had turned brown from front to back all over. It seemed that the cows lost all control of their bodily functions at the point of impact and deposited the results on my car.

Without any warning the engine started to slowly flame up and burn. I opened the trunk for Chris and Lindsey to remove our instruments and clothes. I got cow manure on my hands from getting into the car to remove the 8-track player as I watched the engine burn through the splattered windshield. Luckily the car never exploded. The fire eventually went out of its own accord. The State Troopers showed up. I was standing in the road giving them all the information needed for their report. I asked one of them to please shoot the cows that were injured and obviously dying there in the ditches. He would not end their suffering because he did not want to put in his report that he shot cows. Then, someone else pulled up in a car, people I had never met, people that God had put right in my path, people that God would use to give me a spiritual wake-up call. They were Good Samaritans who were very kind and helpful.

The gentleman in the car, after getting information from me on what happened and who we were, with our permission, loaded our luggage and instruments into his car. He and his wife took our possessions just down the road to a simple house and invited us to come when we had finished up at the scene of the accident, use their phone to call our parents and someone to come pick us up and carry us on into school.

The State Trooper generously took us down to the house as my now-violated car was being towed away. We entered and greeted them. They gave us drinks. We made our phone calls. Conversation began.

"Where are you boys headed?"

"We are students at Brewton-Parker and we were headed back there when this happened."

"What are you studying?"

"We are all ministerial students. I'm studying music."

God must have had the biggest grin on His wonderful face at this point. He had me right where He wanted me. So, we talked about ministry.

They began to share with us that they too, were Christians. We again expressed our appreciation for them taking care of us. Curiosity then overwhelmed me. I realized we were just outside of Milan, Georgia.

Then I just blurted out, "So, where do you go to church?"

The response caused me to almost do a spit take with my soft drink as they replied, "Milan Baptist Church."

At this point in the conversation I should have just quietly sipped my cold drink. Instead, knowing their situation, I asked the question.

"How were your services today?"

Their reply, as it unfolded, shrank me smaller and smaller into my seat. When they finished, I could have walked under a night crawler with a hat on I felt so low and small. God was lovingly pounding my spiritual backside with His rod of correction.

They shared with me that their pastor had suddenly taken ill and was in the hospital. The church could not find anyone to preach in his place at the last minute, so they had a hymn service and then a time of prayer for their pastor that morning, then did the same during the evening service. That sweet couple will never know how God used them to cut me to the core about my attitude toward being a preacher boy, adding speaking and teaching and preaching to my ministry skills. Our ride pulled up into their yard finally and I could not exit fast enough. I was broken. God had gotten through to me. In the days ahead several events would take place. Dad found who owned the cows, and the poor gentleman paid us what he was able in damages to help me purchase another car. Dad returned with money and a jar of sorghum syrup. Mom baked biscuits and we celebrated that weekend. That is also the weekend dad found me another car, a 1965 Chevrolet Impala, bronze, very nice, with a good system in it.

8-tracks were THE thing then.

There was one more event that took place that weekend. I met with Pastor Ken Kicklighter at Bethel Baptist Church. Without any further hesitation I shared all the events that led up to this meeting with him. I asked him if the church would license me to preach! And, they did.

I understand now that life is much simpler if we submit to God's promptings in our lives. When my life gets complicated, I find that almost without exception it is because an area of my life is off in the weeds, totally off-course with God's plan. That has been true in my private life and my ministerial life. For, one area dovetails into the other. If our spiritual life, our personal walk has become undisciplined, it has an effect on our ministry. Likewise, when we get wrapped up in good things, great ministry projects, but things that God is really not into, it will affect the ministry and our personal lives. It complicates things. Rich Mullin wrote a song entitled "Simplify." In the large scope of life and faith, things are much simpler when we seek God first and follow. Often, in the midst of our "stuff" God shows up and it requires us to lay down our "stuff" and go with what God is doing. When we get in the flow of God's activity in His creation, life becomes simpler. I would never say it becomes easier. I would never say it becomes less stressful.

I have discovered through the years that it is much simpler to do things God's way. Why is that true? God knows the end even at the beginning. God always has our best interest at heart. Being in the center of God's purpose for your life is the safest place in the world you can be. I have learned to relax more into God's plan. I have discovered that I can preach, teach, and speak. I approach those times with great respect understanding that purporting to speak on behalf of God is a high and holy thing to do. There is another thing that has been different in my life since that fateful evening when God saw a fence down and saw an opportunity to show His love for me. Since that night, I have had no more encounters with cows on country roads while driving along thinking all is right with the world. Just around the corner from that dramatic moment when metal met leather, was to come an experience beyond my wildest dreams.

CHAPTER FOUR

A MAJOR DREAM COMES TRUE

Childhood dreams know no boundaries. As a kid I would sit in a lounge chair on a warm summer day for hours and just dream. The direction in which my mind went was never in the direction people usually think a young boys' mind would go. While other boys dreamed of being a great NFL quarterback or being a tough police officer, or playing for a Major League team, my dreams were traveling to other places. My dreams told me clearly that I would never be an athlete. I have always enjoyed watching a great sporting event, but I never really wanted to be a player out on that football grid.

My bent was more toward the arts. Music was more and more becoming my passion. My father, understanding this, kept the house filled with this incredible music. He took me to concerts. One memorable concert that my father and I attended was an organ recital by Virgil Fox, a maestro of huge proportions. My mother would drive me for 30 minutes each week to piano lessons. As I would watch a performer onstage my mind would put me up there doing that. I enjoyed watching actors onscreen playing roles and sometimes fantasized that I was in a movie as I would live out a day.

I am not sure when this notion hit me. I just know that at some point one of my dreams became huge. Perhaps God planted this dream in my heart. I wanted to sing for someone really important. Perhaps I could sing one day for the President of the United States. I could think of no more important an audience than to stand in front of the President and sing. To this day I love to sing.

As I entered my teen years I also entered the world of rock music. In the sixth grade I did go out for basketball. One day after practice I got into the car with my mom, Chuck Taylor Cons on and gym shorts and all. I heard something on the radio that mesmerized me. It was the Beatles singing "I Wanna Hold Your Hand." I had never heard music like that before! I proceeded to exit basketball and wrestling to enter into a rock band with my cousin Chris and my friends Dale, David, and Steve. A small step toward God preparing me for something much bigger, we practiced hard. We were serious about making it work. We became High School rock stars eventually, playing for local dances, parties, even winning the local battle of the bands, but getting soundly whipped at the big one!

The experience of being in that band, as negative as it was at times, helped me hone some skills that I would need in the years coming. I learned to play guitar confidently. I developed a vocal style. I learned how to relate to crowds of people from the stage. That was a very important skill that God taught me.

I am a very shy and introverted person. I found it difficult to be in front of people. At my first piano recital in the third grade, I was so terrified of being onstage in front of people, so afraid I would mess up that piano piece, that I balked on the way to the car and began crying. I was a total wreck inside. Mom took me back inside, talked to me, and gave me a very small dose of a sedative that relaxed me just enough to get me through the recital. I remember nights playing dances with the band that during the break I would step outside and throw up I was so nervous. Playing piano at Sycamore Baptist Church and guitar at Bethel Baptist Church helped me gain the confidence I would need for what was to come. Those church experiences also helped me understand that the talents I was using in that band could be also used to bring people closer to God.

I entered the doors of Brewton-Parker College. I auditioned and won a spot with one of the Public Relations music groups called The Folk Four. I was a 12-string guitarist and vocalist. I also was in the Chorus led by Hildegard Stanley, one of the most persistent and gifted directors and musicians I have ever met. She also oversaw The Folk Four. Still shy and covering it with cockiness and bravado, I launched out with that group and performed in front of high schools all over the state of Georgia, and in churches that I cannot even count.

Miss Stanley walked into chorus with a paper in her hand with this look in her face like she had just won the lottery. She sat before us and began to read that piece of paper. I was close enough to see that the piece of paper looked very official. What she read took my breath away. The chorus was invited to join with Baylor University's orchestra and with Colonel Jim Irwin, who walked on the moon, to travel that Christmas to Amman, Jordan and give a command performance of Handel's "Messiah" for His Majesty King Hussein. The electricity and excitement that hit that group of college students was staggering. My final year at that Junior College was off to a start that I least expected. My cousin Chris was my roommate. A freshman, he played bass in the jazz band. He was also in the chorus. We talked for hours about the opportunity.

I dug deep into savings I had squirreled way to pay for the trip. It was a once-in-a- lifetime opportunity. The rehearsals were endless and grueling at times. Miss Stanley was polishing us, rubbing off the rough edges of our sound and performance, and crafting us into a singing unit totally focused on the goal . . . a command performance for a king. The packing, the passport, the rehearsals were all done. This would be the only Christmas I would ever miss being home with my family. I knew that on Christmas Eve I would be in Manger Square in Bethlehem performing. I had never been on an airplane. I was bound from Atlanta to New York, to London, then to Amman. The flight was long. I sat in my seat over the Atlantic thinking. Those childhood dreams were coming true.

The music tour in the Middle East was incredible. We landed in Amman and were escorted to our hotel, the Alcazar. By Jordanian standards it was four-star. By American standards it may have ranked as a two-star hotel. The luck of the draw for roommates that night found me in a hotel room alone in a strange country with a different culture and a different religion, Islam, as the major religion. The bathroom was strange. You showered out in the open. The showerhead and faucets were just on one of the walls. You stood out in the open to shower. The toilet was really a different sight for this South Georgia boy who had never been out of the country. The tank was high on the wall over the seat. You pulled a chain to flush it. Again, there was no privacy.

My bed was clean and comfortable. I was so exhausted that sleep easily took over. A few hours later I found myself sitting straight up in the bed. Was that an air raid siren I was hearing through my sleepiness? No, it sounded like a language. The sun was barely peeping over the horizon. I threw back my curtain. Across the street was a mosque with a minaret, or prayer tower. It was the morning call to prayer being blasted over speakers from the minaret that had startled me awake. As my vision continued to clear, something else attracted my attention.

"Frankie! Frankie! Come to our room! You are not going to believe this!"

The screaming was interspersed with Chris, in a state of panic, banging on my door.

"Dude! You have to come see this! Look out my window!" he loudly insisted.

I hazily dressed more appropriately and went to his room. When I saw what was staring me in the face, my stomach retreated into my gym shorts. This was no way to begin your first day on a music tour in a foreign country. As a peered out his window the cold, gray steel of a mounted machine gun on the roof across from Chris' room was pointed right at me! It was a leftover from the Yom Kippur war. We were one of the first groups to come into the country once the borders opened up.

From Amman, Jordan we crossed over into Israel. I could not believe I was standing there in the country of Jesus' birth, ministry, and death. We crossed a bridge from Jordan to Israel. We exited one bus on the Jordanian side of the bridge, walked across the bridge to our bus on the Israeli side of the border. Passports were checked again. Barbed wire was everywhere. We were not allowed to take pictures in the border area. I can tell you that I saw tanks and military vehicles, soldiers armed to the teeth, and barbed wire.

The Israeli part of the tour was fast-paced. I remember seeing Jericho. I recall the Dead Sea vividly. Against the suggestion of the tour guide, I drank from Jacob's well. I have lived to tell about it. The Mount of Olives was quite an interesting place overlooking Old Jerusalem. Old Jerusalem was filled with people, very narrow streets, open-air markets with Jewish and Palestinian women walking home with live ducks and chickens by the neck for dinner. I saw meat hanging out in the open. Customers were pointing to the pieces of meat they wanted. The butcher cut that piece off the carcass, shooed the flies away, wrapped it in paper, and gave it to them.

We sang in Kibbutz all over Israel. Before one performance we were in a room offstage waiting to perform. A group of Messianic Jewish students had joined us. We almost did not make it onstage when it was time for the concert. We were praying together, singing together, dancing in a circle together, and just worshiping God. It was so intense an experience we all were crying. Jewish people were hugging Americans. The common bond was Christ. That time of worship I carry with me as one of the events in my life where God was powerfully real.

All the concerts in Israel were leading up to Christmas Eve in Manger Square in Bethlehem. This event is broadcast around the world annually. There were lights strung everywhere. There were people dancing in the streets. Some had too much to drink. It was bitterly cold. We were allowed to go to the traditional birthplace of Jesus. It lies under a church. We stooped down through a small door into a cave. The Catholic Church had decorated it with candles and gold. There was the spot where Mary gave birth to Jesus, according to tradition, and another spot where she laid him in the manger. I wept as I prayed thanking God for sending Jesus. I thanked Him for allowing me to see the cave where it is believed our Savior was born. Others around me were wiping tears. But it was time now to step back into the bitter cold and wait until it was our turn to take the risers in Manger Square and sing. We were housed in a school until time for our performance. It was cold. My guitar would not stay tuned. One of our pieces used guitars as accompaniment. My hands were cold, even inside the building, which was not heated. With jackets on, and with my leather gloves in my pocket, we marched single-file toward the risers. The cold hit my face and hands. My hands went numb from the extreme chill. There was only one thing to do. I reached in my pocket, took out my gloves, and put them on! Now, I had another challenge ahead of me. How was I going to play a 12-string in leather gloves? The moment came. I strapped on the guitar, and took a deep breath as Miss Stanley was grinning at me with her arms in the air ready to begin the piece, looking like a hovering bird ready to swoop down on her prey, the choir! Somehow, I managed to get through that piece and play with cold, gloved hands.

It was Christmas Eve. After the concert back at the hotel, I remember the line at the phone as we waited our turn to call home. After a nice bath and a peaceful night's sleep in a warm bed, I slept into Christmas day. After breakfast, we were on our way to the empty tomb. We sang resurrection songs. Col. Jim Irwin spoke of the hope of the resurrection as he stood in front of the entrance to the tomb, another cave. Then, we all filed inside. There was the grave and the place where the body should be was very clean and well-kept. During the course of the tour we had also seen traditional Mt. Calvary. There is to this day a Moslem graveyard up there so we could not go there out of respect for their faith, but we could view the place from a great vantage point. It DID look like a skull.

Again, my dream being fulfilled more and more, there was coming a time when another twist from God himself would propel me into something that I was totally unprepared for. God loves surprises. He loves to give good gifts to his kids. Every surprise God has given me has been incredible and totally undeserved. I am sure God laughs at times at my reaction. We boarded a bus to go back to the border of Jordan and cross over for the main reason we had come, the command performance for His Majesty King Hussein. Again, the soldier on the bus who checked our passports could not get my name right. I was "Flanklin Villea." I dared not laugh at an armed soldier. It was hysterical seeing them wrestle with my name though. Shalom, Israel. Salome, Jordan. God was about to spring his serendipity on me.

We arrived back in Amman and got settled back in the hotel. The time came for us to arrive at the cultural palace where the performance would be for dress rehearsal and sound checks. Baylor's orchestra sounded fantastic. Our 100 voices combined with 40 instruments blended into a sound that George Frederick Handel would be pleased with. The cultural palace was beautiful. The auditorium was spacious. About half-way back was a special box area where King Hussein and his new bride would sit the following evening to enjoy the performance.

As the dress rehearsal concluded, Hildegard Stanley called for the following people to meet with her in the front left section of the auditorium: the people in the hand bell choir, and Michael Holcomb, Deborah Wilcox, Emily Marchman, and Frankie Wiley. As we gathered around her among the seats in that section of the auditorium, I noticed she had a telegram in her hand. What was going on? Had we violated some Islamic code and were being deported back to America? Was there a tragedy at home that we in that group needed to know about? She had a serious look on her face. She announced that there had been a change of plans for us for the approaching evening. Then she opened the telegram. Crown Prince Hassan, the brother of His Majesty King Hussein, requested the honor of our presence at his home to entertain him and his guests and to be his guests for dinner.

I got scared. Surely this was some sick joke or wild dream. The only problems were that she was not joking and I was wide awake. While the rest of the entourage was at a restaurant that evening we were picked up in taxis sent by the Crown Prince and whisked away on a hilly, fast, and bumpy ride to the Crown Prince Hassan's palace. I don't remember any conversation in the taxi. I believe we were all too stunned at what we were about to do.

We were greeted at the palace by the Protocol Officer and soldiers. Our guitar cases and bell cases were searched for bombs and weapons, which I completely understood. We were then graciously ushered inside by the P O and into a private room. There, he instructed us on how we should address His Majesty and how we were to conduct ourselves while at the palace. When the prince stood, we were to stand. When the prince sat, we were to sit. The only exception to the rule was while we were performing. We were not allowed to "evangelize." Knowing that we were Christians and would perform Christian songs, we were allowed to sing the songs but could not seek to convert the prince who saw himself as a direct descendent of the prophet Mohammed. We could not show the soles of our feet. As we sat, we were to keep our feet flat on the floor. In Islamic culture, to show the soles of your shoes is a tremendous insult. From there we were led to the area of our performance. The bell choir completed their concert. It was our turn.

A shy, introverted kid from a small town in South Georgia who spent his summers dreaming of singing for someone important found himself at nineteen years old standing in front of an heir apparent to the throne of Jordan. Seated with the prince and his lovely wife were royalty from all over Europe and the Middle East. There were other princes, dukes, duchesses, and people with titles there I had never heard of. We launched into our set. We began with the "secular" songs and then moved to a few Christian songs with no introduction to them as such . . . until we came to the song "I Wish We'd All Been Ready." I decided this song needed explanation. I was about to walk a thin line of proper protocol.

"In America most of us believe as Christians. The song we are about to sing expresses a particular belief of Christians that Jesus will one day return and take Christians to heaven. It further encourages Christians to be prepared for that day. Enjoy!"

I did it! No one arrested me. I was not shot immediately. I had managed to share my faith with a direct descendant of the prophet Mohammed and a person of royalty without being offensive. As we sang, the prince smiled and nodded his approval. That was our final song. There was warm and genuine applause. The prince then invited us to join him and his guests for dinner.

What I saw in the dining hall was a buffet-style spread of food that makes Golden Corral look like the Dwarf House. There was so much food I hardly knew where to begin. The food was good. It was well-prepared. The prince was so kind and gracious to us. After the meal he invited us to join him in the parlor. I could not believe my eyes. The walls were woodworked shelves with vinyl albums of music filling them. The prince enjoyed jazz. He played some of his favorite recordings for us, a great host. Cigar in hand he sat with us as we listened to music and he asked us about our trip to Jordan and Israel. The evening seemed in my mind to last forever. God granted me my dream in a surprising and unexpected way. The time came for us to say goodbye and return to the hotel. As he stood, we stood also. We gathered on one side of the room facing the prince and his wife. As our goodbye to him, we all sang:

> "Goodbye. Our God is watching o'er you.
> Goodbye. His presence goes before you.
> Goodbye and we'll be praying for you, So,
> goodbye. May God bless you."

As we sang I saw tears in the Prince's eyes. He wished us well, shook our hands, and we left the palace and returned to our hotel. It was a night I could hardly sleep. I was still trying to process and understand what had just happened. I had been the recipient of the grace and blessing of God beyond my wildest expectations. And God was not finished with me. The next day held an even larger fulfillment of those boyhood dreams. I finally drifted to sleep knowing that an insecure boy from a nothing town in South Georgia was greatly loved by God. The final chapter of this trip was coming tomorrow. Why would God allow such an awesome event in such a guy's life? His unconditional love for me is the reason.

The next day we arrived at the cultural palace for final sound checks and preparation for the big event. His Majesty King Hussein had just returned from his honeymoon marriage to an American that day. The plan was for Col. Jim Irwin to speak and to present a rock from the moon to the king. Afterward we would perform Handel's MESSIAH. As the choir filed onstage to begin the performance there he was in the center of the auditorium dressed in full regalia, his new bride at his side. The moon rock had been presented. The orchestra began the overture. We sang with every breath in us. When

"The Hallelujah Chorus" began, the audience rose to their feet in keeping with the traditions attached to that piece.

I felt my heart rising into my throat at the same moment. Each time I have sung that piece I have sung the hallelujahs with passion. This night I had to take it up a notch. This was the dream become reality. This was the summer afternoon in a lounge chair where a 12 year-old dreamed of singing for someone like this, a president or a king. Only now I was 19. Seven years later, the 12 year-old's summer fantasy had come true in a foreign country called Jordan, the city of Amman, in front of the king of that sovereign nation.

CHAPTER FIVE

EXPECT THE UNEXPECTED FROM GOD

The evangelism team was made up of Bill Hardee, Dixie Maddox, Jill Usery, and me. We were four young college students out to change the world for God. We had the passion, the strength, the youth, and the boldness to do it . . . or so we thought. Brewton-Parker College sent out these teams for weekend student revivals. Our team had not been sent and I was like a horse in the starting gate ready to run the race.

I began to fast about this lack of opportunity of service. It was the first time I had ever gone without food and spent time before the Lord when I could be in the cafeteria or at Judy's making a pig of myself. I could not understand. Why was God not letting us do revivals? We were all Christians. We had the talents to do it. We had the desire. For three days I fasted before the Lord on behalf of the team. At breakfast, I would go to the cafeteria and get water or orange juice and chat for a moment with friends, then head to the dorm for some time alone. That scenario would repeat itself during lunch and dinner for three days. I read Scripture. I searched my life. I prayed. I had never been so serious and passionate before the Lord.

On the fourth day, I sleepily crawled out of bed, grunted a "good morning" to Ron, my roommate, and headed for the showers to shave and wash the sleep away. I went to breakfast to intentionally break the fast. I sensed that there was no need for further fasting. I ate a titanic breakfast. It was a wonderful experience. College cafeteria food had never tasted so delectable. I chatted with some friends around the table, laughing and talking about nothing really. I have no recollection of what that conversation was about. I just remember it was good to be eating again.

I looked at my watch and saw that I needed to begin walking back to the dorm to retrieve my books for class. It was a walk across half the campus. My dormitory was shaped like a horseshoe. Near the sidewalk at the open front of that building were telephones. I passed by on my way to my room, situated to the right and front leg of that horseshoe-shaped building. The phone rang. I turned back on a whim and answered the phone. God was already smiling I am sure. The voice in my ear asked for Frankie. The voice was that of an older man. "Speaking, "I replied.

What I heard next caused my heart to leap into my throat. I could hardly breathe at first. On the other end of that conversation was Pierce Wilcox, then pastor of Pinecrest Baptist Church in Cordele, GA. He invited the team to come lead a weekend spring revival at his church for their teenagers. After a good conversation I hung up the phone, went to class and could not wait to get with Bill, Dixie, and Jill, who were in agreement that we could take this one. No scheduling conflicts were there among us. I called Pastor Wilcox and told him we would come and also got more information on what he wanted us to do.

We arrived in Cordele on that spring day, a Friday, to an atmosphere that was tense, confusing, and foreboding. We passed a street on our way to Pastor Wilcox's home that was packed with cars. The whole scene before us as we drove into town was screaming that things were far beyond normal for that sleepy little South Georgia town. God had walked us into a situation that forced us to wrestle with Him all over again.

Pastor Wilcox met us at the door of his home with his wife, Martha Jane, just behind him. Both of them had looks of utter devastation on their faces. After greetings and we were seated, I asked what the meaning of all the cars were in that neighborhood we had seen in passing. Pastor Wilcox dropped his head, looked at us, and said, "I need to talk to you all about that."

He began to unfold a most horrific thing that came to pass that week. Three people were dead and a woman was injured at the hands of a teenaged boy. Jerry, a senior student at Crisp County High School, had gone berserk in his home and murdered his father, his grandfather, his sister, and wounded his mother. I was feeling nauseous. Bill's face was pale. The girls were speechless. The whole community was in shock.

Jerry was an honor student. He was president of the Beta Club. I came to understand that he could shoot a basketball from half court and strip the net with hardly an effort. It made no sense to me that a person with so much positive in his life would resort to such a heinous act. Pastor Wilcox looked at us sadly as his wife stood there crying. "What do you want to do?" he asked. "You can go on back to college if you wish and forget this weekend, or you can try it tonight and see how the service goes, then decide if you want to continue. But I do not see how we can have a youth revival right now", he softly and sadly spoke. Bill and I looked at each other, each waiting for the other to speak.

Bill then spoke what I was feeling in my heart but too afraid to risk verbalizing. I was sitting there thinking that God did not put us here by accident. Bill affirmed that. We decided to go ahead with the Friday night service and see what the mood of the students was. And so, we began to move to the church for that service. God was smiling again, I am sure.

The Friday night meeting was dire. The students sat like zombies frozen with eyes fixed on nothing. Their resistance was obvious. The questions in their minds were not being addressed. The music did not move them. Bill struggled through a message that fell on deaf ears and hearts. They were grieving and looking for answers. Where was God in all of this tragedy? Why would God allow such a terrible thing to happen? Can I even trust God? I could hear in my mind all these questions from these kids. Why? I could hear them because I had some of the same questions going on in my mind. The altar call left the altar just as vacant after the call as before. No one budged. Why should they? They were mad at God.

Bill often scared me. He could be so bold for God. Sometimes I thought he was just stupid with some of the things he did, but I learned from Bill to come out of my shyness at least long enough to show some Godly courage. Bill scared me again after the service. We were talking about what to do. I was honestly discouraged and ready to pack up and go back to Brewton-Parker College and forget that this weekend ever happened. Bill had another idea. When I was just about to say that we should pack up and head out Bill stopped me cold with one sentence. "We should go see Jerry." My haughty response was, "What did you just say?" He repeated it. He wanted to go to the jail and see Jerry and try to win him to Christ. I thought Bill had lost his mind, and then God spoke to my heart about how selfish I was being, so I repented of my attitude. Pastor Wilcox made a call to the sheriff. Bill, Pastor Wilcox, and I had an appointment with a teenaged murderer on Saturday morning at 9:00.

I wrestled with God all night that Friday into Saturday morning. I could not sleep. God was hammering my heart into a heart that would break for such a person as Jerry, because God's heart surely was broken. In that room that night at one point I know I saw angels surrounding my bed giving me assurance and peace that God knew what He was doing. It was a presence I cannot even put into words, but they were there. Night brightened into morning and we were on our way to the jail while the students from the church were at the little mall in Cordele to sing and pass out flyers about the revival.

The courthouse was your typical small-town government building. The jail was small but well-kept, a jail I would eventually visit several more times. We were led to his cell, but not allowed inside with him. We were to visit with him through the bars. There he was, a typical 17 year old. He was blonde and handsome with an innocence about him that belied the fact that he was in jail on charges of murder three times over. He was sad. Bill and Pastor Wilcox did the talking. God had me there to learn a lesson. The conversation quickly moved to spiritual things when we shared with him why we were in town and why we came to the jail. Bill and Pastor Wilcox began sharing the hope of Jesus with him and how a person can receive forgiveness because of Jesus' death on the cross. Jerry was listening. His eyes were glistening with tears. I was praying for him. Jerry was so ready to trust Jesus as his Savior and receive forgiveness, something he had never done.

Eight hands through bars joined together. Words of the sinner's prayer were spoken. A young man behind bars charged with murder became washed clean in the blood of the Lamb. Jerry was a child of God. We rejoiced together and encouraged him in his new faith. I was blown away. I began to understand. As we left the jail to join the students at the little mall, our shock at what God had done turned to excitement and expectation of what was next.

We arrived and gathered those students together and broke the news to them. Before my very eyes, the icy cold in their eyes melted into tears of joy. The ashen faces of those kids began to color with new hope. They were crying and laughing and telling people around them all that happened that morning at the Crisp County Jail.

They sang with all their heart. God was working a miracle. God was about to glorify Himself through the most tragic event I had experienced at the time. This was not at all what I expected.

We prayed and prepared for the Saturday night service. There was no way we were going home now. God was on a roll! We wanted to hang out and see what would happen next. I felt Spirit-filled and confident in God as I sang. Dixie and Jill were wonderful with the little children and their musical contributions to the team. Bill spoke quietly as was his nature, but powerfully under an anointing I had not seen before. God was doing a thing!

The altar call was given. For 20 minutes teenagers flowed to and from the altar, praying, repenting, finding Jesus real for the first time, "getting saved," as Baptists like to say, and just ministering to one another, praying together in groups. Healing was going on in those hearts that, the night before, were broken and bruised and questioning God. Bill and I wept at the sight. We prayed with them and loved on them and encouraged them for some time. But the miracles were not over. There was one more person God had in mind in Cordele that night. It was time for that teenager to meet God in a powerful way right there in front of his friends.

Down near Interstate 75 is a Dairy Queen restaurant to this day in Cordele. Being hungry and thirsty after such a grueling day we rode there for a burger and a Coke. Bill, Dixie, Jill, and I were sitting and talking over the day and about the incredible meeting we had just experienced. Some teenaged boys in a nearby booth were listening to every word we said. These boys had the spirit, just not the Holy Spirit. They were obviously drunk. One of them in a drunken and slurred voice yelled out, "Come over here and tell us about Jesus."

Bill scared me sometimes. He got up and went over to them with me not far behind. Bill greeted them with "Yes, I will tell you about Jesus." Those inebriated teens began to laugh and make fun of us and our Jesus. Then Bill scared me again. Bill asked a question that nearly made me want to run for the door. In his soft-spoken way he asked, "Why don't I pray and ask God to sober you up? Do you believe He can do that?" One boy there raised his hand and said, "I believe."

Bill bowed and prayed, asking God to sober that young man up so that he could clearly hear the plan of salvation. When the boy raised his head I am not sure who was more amazed, him or me. His eyes had gone from an alcohol-soaked red to clear, and he was sober! Bill took him aside and we shared how to be saved. He accepted Christ that night. When the other boys saw him praying to receive Christ, they really let up a howl of intimidation and ridicule because he was going to be a "Jesus Freak." Bill and I shared some things to help him get started in his walk with God. He got up to leave, and the boys were still wailing on him with insults. He stopped in the door of the Dairy Queen, looked right at that table of boys, and said, "Don't knock it until you have tried it." With that he left and I never saw him again. I have a hunch that this guy was an influence on many others coming to Christ in that school. It had been a day of miracles.

We finished up the service Sunday and then headed back to Mt. Vernon. Bill was driving and I was thinking. With God you can expect the unexpected. We had the idea we would go to a nice little town and do a nice little weekend revival and save a few teenaged souls and enjoy singing and preaching and doing what we like to do. God had other plans. I know that the fasting I did was part of God's preparation for me to face what I had faced. In the fasting I learned to listen to God. I learned to try to see what God is about and go with Him. I learned that I had to be taught some things. God used Bill Hardee and Pastor Wilcox and Jerry to teach me to see things from God's perspective. When I was ready to go home, God was ready to reveal His power and purpose for us being there. God taught me through Bill that weekend that it is okay to be bold when you know you are in God's will and hands. Bill just naturally seemed to flow with what God was doing. I learned that ministry is often messy and even ugly. There are times in ministry when real life shows up and you are called on to respond with the love of God, unconditionally. I did not want to go see Jerry. He was a murderer. There was no love in that attitude. God loved him, even though he killed three people. God showed me that I too could love those not so loveable. That Saturday morning in that jailhouse, God began to move my heart from conditional love to unconditional love.

It's easy to love teenagers when everything is cool and normal. When they are not so cool calls on student pastors to "up the love" and show them that you love them no matter what they do or what they say. My culture had taught me to be conditional in my love for people. As long as they do what I want them to do, as long as they don't hurt me, as long as they play my game, I could love them. That was easy. The words of Jesus come back to haunt me when I think of my attitude in those days. He was not so kind to the Pharisees, who loved conditionally. I was no better than them. Jesus said that it is easy to love those who love you and play the game. What reward is there in that? Real love is shown when we love those who are not so loveable. Jesus' words and Jesus' life and death for me are living proof that it is true sacrifice to God to love those who are not so nice. As God's child I had to learn to love people no matter what. That love has gotten me through some difficult times down through the years in ministry. Unfortunately, I have seen that church members can be some of the meanest people on the face of the earth. How do you love people who do not like your ministry? How do you love people who call you to minister your gifts because they know that you are equipped in that area of ministry, and then proceed to tell you how to do your job? How do you love people who smile to your face while they are unraveling your ministry behind your back? How do you love church members who will outright lie about you? How do you love deacons who stand in a business meeting and call your pastor every name in the book except a gentleman? How do you love the teenager who physically slams you into the wall every time he walks by you at church? How do you love the 16 year-old boy who comes to church but won't get out of his truck and come to youth meeting, sitting there high until the meeting is over? How do you love the girl who is giving her body to any guy that wants it? How do you love the girls who begin a feud in the 7th grade and continue the feud past their high school graduation? How do you love the girls who gossip about everyone when they are just as guilty and ruin the reputations of adult leadership? I have seen that done to some fellow ministers.

The questions can go on for a long time. Every question I raised above I have experienced personally or seen fellow ministers have to confront in their ministries. The answer is simple but not easy. You love people unconditionally. That is what Jesus did. It killed him. Even while he was dying on the cross, he was loving people unconditionally. He prayed for the very ones who put him on the cross. At the point of my Cordele experience God began to teach me that I had to stop loving people as long as they were kind to me and did things my way, as long as they were not sinners . . . or murderers.

I began to put that into practice immediately. I certainly needed the practice. I would practice unconditional love for years to come and still not get it completely down! But I began with an accused triple murderer in a jail in Cordele. That town was on the way home to Sycamore. I began to write Jerry from college. My letters were to just encourage him to stay strong in his faith. On weekends when I was headed home and could,

I began to stop at the jail and visit with him for a few minutes. I began to learn to love the ones that were not loveable. I began to see that Jerry's life was still worth something to God. I began to understand that the good boy from South Georgia needed grace just as much as the mass murderer. I met his mom one day at the jail. She stays in my mind as an incredible woman. She stood by Jerry through the trial, his time in a mental institution, and then took him with her to California after he was deemed fit to return to society. At that point I lost touch with them. He may never remember me if we were to meet again. I will never forget him and the lesson in unconditional love he taught me.

CHAPTER SIX

THE FIGHT BETWEEN THE BOY AND THE MAN

I have heard more evangelists preach than I care to even remember. There is an inside joke among pastors that all you have to do to be an evangelist is write seven sermons, buy seven flashy suits, and that's it. You go to one place and preach your seven sermons, and then you go to the next place and repeat them. Generally, I have had little use for evangelists down through the years. The one evangelist that I have nothing but admiration and respect for is Billy Graham. And though I have little use for the flash and pomp and circus-like antics of such evangelists as Earnest Angsley, Benny Hinn, and other such TV evangelists, one Southern Baptist evangelist said something that I have never forgotten and it impacted my life greatly.

I have no recollection of where I was when I heard Jay Strack preach. What he said has never left me. It opened my eyes to my own state, and caused me to make some changes, to be more conscious of my behavior and my life. I have walked a thin line as a student pastor between acting as an adult should act as a good role model for teens, and acting like a teen myself. I think that is a difficult balance for a student pastor. You want to relate to them and engage them in activities they enjoy. After years of wrestling with this issue in my life I came to understand some things.

"There comes a time when the boy has to sit down and the man has to stand up!" Those were the words of Jay Strack that have never left me. My 20's were years of the battle between the boy in me and the man in me. In my life, the boy constantly wanted to come out and play. But I came to understand that there were times when you could not tell the student pastor from the students. The man in me was crying out for his time, but at times I enjoyed the boy so much that the man was neglected.

My 20's were years of finishing my bachelor's degree at Shorter College, stepping out for the first time into a full-time staff position at Second Avenue Baptist Church, then heading off to Southern Baptist Theological Seminary, then once again filling a position at Rehoboth Baptist Church and turning full-circle back to Second Avenue Baptist Church. There was much flux going on. It was a period of time when I was making up my mind once and for all about some life decisions. It was time for the boy to sit down and the man to stand up.

I transferred to Shorter College after completing my Associate's Degree at Brewton-Parker College. It was there that I completed my Bachelor's Degree in Church Music. I became a brother of Phi Mu Alpha, the professional music fraternity. I sang in the chorale, a select group of vocal students. I performed lead roles in two major operas. I was driving 30 minutes one way on weekends to Roland Springs Baptist Church to lead worship and work with their kids. I took on the Associate Directorship of the Rome Boys Club Choir. I traveled with the Shorter College Pop Group. I also found time to actually attend class. Much of Shorter is a blur in my mind today. I passed my piano proficiencies, did my senior recital well and enjoyed my time at Shorter.

My vocal professor was Dr. Bob Jones, who is not related to the Bob Jones of that university in Tennessee. Dr. Jones has had an influence on my life that I never fully understood until much later in life. Dr. Jones pulled notes out of me that I never dreamed I had inside. My range jumped to five octaves under his coaching. He, being the director of the Rome Boys Club Choir, put me on his staff as the Associate. He called me to his office one day and involved me in a conversation regarding my job at Rowland Springs. My objection to that position was the driving. He told me that his church, Second Avenue Baptist Church, was looking for someone to work with their students. In just a few weeks I became their part-time student minister. Here I was in one of the larger congregations in Rome, Georgia as a staff member and not out of college. And so began a relationship with a group of loving people, tough at times, but loving nonetheless.

It was there that I met students who now are married with children and send me pictures of their kids, my "grandkids" as some of them have called their children. It was at this place that I honed my skills as a musician as well as a student pastor. The battle between the boy and the man continued. In my inexperience I believed that the best way to win students and relate to them was to act like them. There is nothing sadder than an immature college student. Not only was the man in me trying to emerge once and for all, but that little boy in me really liked to come out and play, and being a student pastor allows you to do some really fun things that allow the kid to come out. At those times it is appropriate. Keeping a balance between the boy and the man requires wisdom. Knowing the difference between being child-like and childish is important also. I came to discover that students to this day are not looking for someone to act like them and be their buddy. They do not need that from adults. Deep inside their hearts, students are looking for men and women they can look up to and draw strength and guidance from, not a post-adolescent playmate.

My position at Second Avenue Baptist Church was taken, knowing that upon my graduating Shorter, the position would be full-time. At the time I had no intention of doing any post-graduate work. The degree was conferred, the job became full-time, and I had to find a place to live. What I found was humble, cheap, and beginning to fall apart. Out a road in Floyd County was a single-wide trailer owned by a little lady who rented it for money, which I am sure she needed to live. She was always very kind to me. I could not say the same for the home she rented to me. It was furnished. All I had to buy was a little portable TV. The couch cushions were showing signs of wear. The tile floor had seen better days. The air conditioning unit was stuck through the window on the living room end of the trailer, and propped up with a long board. Air leaked in big time around the unit. When a good breeze blew the unit would sway slightly. In the winter, the trailer would get so cold that I would turn the oven on some nights in addition to the heating unit to get the temperature comfortable inside. Cold air rushed right in around that air conditioning unit.

Thankfully, the oven worked. The man really stood up when I had to feed myself. I learned quickly how to cook. Eventually I moved into another trailer that was warm and still affordable and had plenty of room. And the full-time ministry began to blossom. Kids started bringing kids. They began showing up in my office just to chat, then to talk about more serious things. There are some things they share that are so very serious to them. But to you as an adult, you are sitting there listening intently and seriously on the outside, while on the inside you are laughing so hard you think you will explode. Such an event happened to me when 13 year old Mark walked into my office. He shut the door behind him as he entered, looked at me and said, "Can I ask you a question?" I assured him he could ask me anything. I was not prepared for this one. It was a chance for the boy to really come out, but thankfully the man took over in me and helped Mark make sense out of his question.

He sat down and it almost seemed he was tearing up to cry. He began to share with me how, at school, he was uncomfortable. When asked to explain that, he painfully and hesitantly shared that after gym class in the showers that he had noticed he was not as "developed" as the others. He wanted to know if something was wrong with him. Was Mark physically all right?

I remember taking a deep breath. Inside the boy was rolling in the floor laughing at such a question. The man breathed a prayer to God for wisdom. Then I told Mark not to worry. I shared with him how God has put within each of us our own special timetable for things to happen to our bodies. Each timetable is different. For some, physical growth happens at 11. For others physical growth comes at 13 or 14. God would allow Mark to grow soon, and it would be right on time, according to God's timetable for Mark. I told him to be patient. He would grow up normal and healthy in God's plan for him. This child breathed a huge sigh of relief. He looked at me and grinned. At that moment I knew I had gotten through to him. He left my office and closed the door. I put my hand over my mouth until I knew he was out of earshot. Then I spent about 2 minutes laughing so hard my stomach hurt.

The man was standing up. In that group of students were Dr. Jones' kids, a really precious boy named Tommy, Ann, Ben, Barry, and so many others. We had some great times doing talent shows with Mike doing his dead-on Elton John impression. Trips to Six Flags were almost sacred events. There were times on Lake Weiss, and beach retreats. There were times I got to share my heart and what I knew of Scripture with them. This church was alive.

I involved myself in dramas they performed. I sang in the choir there, which was one of the best I have ever heard. I never knew Baptist churches even knew about Dubois' "The Seven Last Words of Christ," much less would sing it! Dr. Jones set high standards and it paid off. During my time at Second Avenue I learned to set high standards. I learned I had to grow up. I learned that I had much to learn about the vocation God was drawing me into. Those three years of full-time ministry there helped me sort out a lot of things about my life and its direction. It grew me up. It gave me respite from having to study and make the grade in a school. I was having so much fun and the group was growing. I was really beginning to get my stride. Then the intercom line in my office rang and Dr. Day, my pastor wanted to spend some time with me.

I walked down the hall to his office and flopped down in a chair. Dr. Day was a great pastor to me. He knew I was young. He knew I had made some mistakes in how I ministered to kids at times. Dr. Day always loved me, regardless of the mess I may have made of an event or said or done something that hurt a kid or a parent. We talked about my ministry there and how well it was going. He was very positive with me and shared with me how much he had seen me grow in ministry. He asked me if I had considered going on for further education in a seminary. My honest answer was no. He told me it that it is something I should think about. He told me that he would love to keep me on his staff, that there was no problem, but that if I was to ever go to graduate school I needed to do it very soon. The longer I put it off, the easier it would be to never take that step. I told him I would give it much thought.

I began to gather information from the Southern Baptist seminaries. I narrowed it down to The Southern Baptist Theological Seminary in Louisville, KY. I applied and was accepted, to the horror of my parents, who thought that my education was done. How would I pay for it? Why was I doing this? I said goodbye to the wonderful people of Second Avenue Baptist Church, at least for the time, loaded up the orange Plymouth Volare, and headed to Louisville with my parents behind me helping me move. Mom was mom. She cried all the way up there, during the whole time we moved me into my dorm, and dad told me later she cried all the way back to Georgia. What is it with mothers? To this day I am not sure if it was the further separation she was feeling, the worry I would not make it, or what. One thing I never doubted was her love for me. I moved into the dorm of the Kentucky Baptist Nursing School across the way from the Baptist hospital there. There were two floors of girls, and a bottom floor of overflow seminary students. What a combination! I must say I dated a few of the girls there, which again was a battle for the boy to sit down and the man to stand up. I was on the verge of three years that would totally reshape me, that would stretch me to the limit, and that would begin to teach me how precious my family really was. It was three years of saying goodbye to the boy and giving the man in me his proper place. I would leave totally different than when I came.

One of my dilemmas that Dr. Day pointed out to me was this. My struggle was not going to be WHAT to do. Because God had gifted me in so many areas, my struggle was to figure out how to roll it all up in a ball and use it all in a ministry. And that has always been my dilemma. Seminary was a place where I could begin to figure that out. Seminary did not teach me practical nuts and bolts of ministry. If one were looking for a "how-to" course in ministry, seminary was not the place for that.

What seminary did was give me tools. I learned disciplines of study in Scripture that have been helpful in preparing to speak to and teach students. I gained new tools to help me dig into the Bible deeper than ever before. I gained insight into the mind of the student. I began to understand principles of religious education that would be valuable to me in the future. I came away with a profound respect for God's Word like I had never known.

I also left Louisville after three years understanding clearly that Christians can be some of the meanest people in the world. I took a job at a small country church in south Louisville near Bullet County and Fort Knox. You could hear the guns and bombs during maneuvers at Fort Knox we were so close. Penile Baptist Church was a strange mixture of people. I had never dealt with hillbillies before. This church was made up of down-to-earth people, for the most part very wonderful people, but people who were products of a clandestine mentality. These were people able to separate God from church "business." It was a shock to me. Not since my teenaged skirmish with the people at Sycamore Baptist Church had I seen church people act so mean and rude and un-Christian. I am not sure to this day what had happened between Pastor House and the church prior to my arrival, but it was clear there was history. Every business meeting was tense. Worship was uncomfortable. Pastor House was an elderly gentleman and very loving and kind, the statesman type. And then there was an older man in the church I will call Earl. Earl was a giant of a man. His face showed the toughness of his life as a railroad man. His hands were huge and rough. He wore overalls and a white shirt to church. And Earl had definite issues. Earl figured Penile Baptist Church belonged to him. It was his church.

I remember a business meeting where Earl stood red in the face and called Pastor House everything but a gentleman. My stomach sank. My heart raced. I wanted to punch him out. Pastor House graciously and with more class than I was feeling at the time, responded firmly but lovingly. It was not enough. Eventually Pastor House and his wife Artie had to leave. It began to sink in that I was now the only staff person at that church. The interim they hired only came Sundays and Wednesdays to preach. The balance of ministry in that church was up to me. I trembled at the thought of a business meeting where I would be the target of Earl's wrath now that the pastor was gone. Something had to give. How would I ever co-exist with Earl?

I began to commit Saturdays to visiting in the community around the church. I made it a point to always stop at Earl's for two reasons: to talk to him and let him talk, and his wife's apple pies. We would sit in the kitchen and talk. I would listen as Earl would relate his feelings about the church, incidents from his life, and not respond to what he said. I listened. Underneath that coarse exterior, I discovered a man who loved his church deeply in the only way he knew. Over apple pie and coffee, we would talk about the church. I eventually began to respond slowly and carefully with my own thoughts. I shared how everyone loves their church. I began to share how when we feel passionately about something we tend to defend it at all costs. I shared my teen skirmish with Sycamore Baptist Church and how the attack on me in a business meeting really hurt me deeply. I began to share over time how the way we respond to things about church that disturb us can help or hurt us and the church. I saw Earl change. I did not share all of these things with him at once. Over time I built a relationship with him that allowed me share some truth with him and allowed him to really hear what I was trying to say. I loved Earl even though he ran my pastor off. I loved Earl even though he put me in a position I was not ready for. I loved Earl unconditionally. Earl never stirred up another controversy for the remainder of the three years I served that church.

There was a funny group of students in that church. June and Joe Fenton were brother and sister. June was a typical blonde. I would tell a funny story in a Bible study and the group would laugh, then 10 minutes later June would start laughing and blurt out, "Oh! I get it!" Joe was the typical young jock. There was Theresa. There was Damon. These and others made up a fun group. One Sunday evening as I led the music, I noticed that all the kids were on the back row instead of scattered with parents as they usually sat on Sunday evenings. Thinking nothing of it, I began the evening service. Pastor House was on the front pew and the pianist was positioned where she could not see the back row. On the last verse of the first hymn, all the students disappeared behind the pew in front of them for a second. When they arose they were holding a long sign done on butcher paper that said, "Frank, your fly is open." Well, being taking off-guard I took a step back from the pulpit and looked down to check. The students were laughing silently on the back row and I knew they had me! Fly closed, I ended the hymn and called on one of our deacons, Mr. Dennis, to pray, which was not in the order of service. I positioned myself on the bench behind the pulpit and proceeded to totally crack up laughing during the prayer. On the "amen" I stood and continued the service. After the service the students were all smug because they got me. After "chewing them out" for such behavior in a worship service we all had a good-natured laugh.

Sue Dennis in that church taught me something very special. Sue was a Down syndrome person, one of the most precious people I have ever met. Sue was 18. Sue had a job on Sunday mornings with her Sunday school class. The teacher would check roll and give it to Sue who would bring it to me in the assembly area outside the student's classrooms. One Sunday, Sue slowly came out of the girls' classroom with the records and closed the door. She started crying as she stood there looking at me. I asked her to come and sit with me. Weeping, she came over and I gave her a hug, offered her a seat and asked her why she was so sad. It is rare to see a Down's syndrome child unhappy. That has been my experience. They are always smiling and loving people. Sue finally got herself together and shakily told me this: "I could not check that I studied my lesson today because my parents were out late at a party and mom did not have time to read me my lesson." Sue's mom faithfully read her the lesson every Saturday night. This one weekend was a very rare exception. Sue's parents were very loving and kind Christian people seeking to raise Sue to know the Lord. I told Sue that I understood and no one was angry with her for that. We loved her. Sue began to smile and I walked her back to her class. Sue made me think that perhaps we should all be as committed to learning about God and the Bible to the point that we cry if we miss times we can study and learn about God. I will never forget Sue Dennis. She is a precious jewel from God who shined brightly while I knew her. She loved unconditionally. She was full of life. I salute her parents for being so careful to let Sue know about the God who created her and loves her.

Three years in Louisville passed swiftly. I could now read Greek and Hebrew. I had tools to study God's Word like never before. I was a much more disciplined person. I had a pretty clear idea now of how I would combine all my talents and abilities from God to minister to students. It would not be just music after all. God had broken through to me. I was to use my musical gifts as another tool to reach students for Jesus.

Graduation time drew near. I wanted desperately to return to Georgia and "get on with it." I missed my family. During my three years at Southern, I lost my grandfather Wiley whom I loved dearly. He helped teach me to fish . . . and to curse. Those two things seemed to go together for him. He never really used profanity unless he was in the boat on the pond with his line snagged. Mom tells a story of the first time she heard me utter profanity that supposedly gave God a last name. I remember vaguely a big blue bar of Zest soap that thoroughly washed my mouth out. My parents knew I picked it up from Granddaddy Wiley because that kind of language was not spoken in our home. There were a few times I was able to fly home while he was in the hospital dying. My dad would meet me at the Macon airport and drive me the rest of the way in. Most times I would just sit by his bed and hold his hand. I did tell him how much I loved him. I flew home for the funeral and I remember walking the streets in my neighborhood as the sun was setting talking to God about my Granddad and how much I was going to miss him. This was another step in the man standing up and fully taking charge.

My resume was circling in Georgia. I remember one evening the hall phone ringing in the dorm. The voice on the other end said, "This is Lester Buice from Rehoboth Baptist Church in Tucker." I honestly almost fainted. The revered pastor of one of the first mega-churches in Georgia was calling me offering me a position as their youth pastor as soon as I graduated. I told him that I was open to talk with them about that. I hung up the phone and nearly got sick at my stomach. I could not believe how God was looking after me.

I graduated seminary with a Master of Divinity in Religious Education. Penile Baptist Church threw me a going-away party. I was headed to Rehoboth. We had all gotten through it. There was Earl, white shirt and overalls, coming down the receiving line. He took my hand tightly. Choking back tears he looked me in the eye. I am not fully sure what he meant by what he said, but I have an idea it was an apology. He said, "You were right, Frankie. You were right." Unconditional love changes the hearts of men.

CHAPTER SEVEN

IT'S ABOUT PEOPLE

I want to begin introducing you to some teenagers. Each of these students during my years at Rehoboth were unique people with individual needs, hurts, and personalities. I do not think one can lump all teenagers into a single category and say, "That is what a teenager is." It was at this place that God, through teenagers, showed me that the world I had imagined they lived in was nothing like I thought.

I had grown up in a stable, Godly home with both parents who loved me and always sought what was best for my life. I lived "Leave It To Beaver." I discovered quickly that while I was away in college and seminary that Wally and the Beaver did not live here anymore. I encountered more dysfunction and hurt than I ever dreamed possible in teenagers' lives. God was about to rock my world. Through my inexperience and mistakes God showed me a lot of grace. I was green. I had never seen such a humongous church and so many teenagers. Each Wednesday night, the "youth building" was packed out with oftentimes over 100 teenagers.

It was 1981. I had formed a band. SKYRIDER was the house band for the meeting and we rocked the place with the latest in contemporary Christian music. Word got out and students were coming from all over. The band would play a mini-concert each week and I would lead a Bible study. We saw many come to Christ. For a time the meeting was even broadcast on a local Christian radio station. I felt totally unprepared for this. Out of that crowd of kids I began forming personal relationships with many of them. I love them to this day, and I am still in contact with many of them who are now married and have children of their own who are almost teenagers. I call their kids my grandchildren. They do, too. I have received e-mails with pictures of my "grandchildren" attached.

One of the first kids I met there was Andy. He was the oldest son of two boys. His younger brother was Ray. I met Andy at church. Andy's mother struggled hard to raise them alone. Their father had left them a long time ago. Andy was 12 when we met. I loved him at first sight. He was tall for his age with sandy blonde hair, green eyes, and rosy cheeks, which gave him a look of innocence that really belied reality!

There was a phone call one morning. Andy had been admitted to Grady Hospital's burn unit, an excellent unit. He was camping out with a group and slept too close to the campfire. His sleeping bag ignited during the night and Andy had third-degree burns on his feet as a result. I drove to Grady Hospital to visit him and pray with him. This was new. The worst hospital visit I had made was when Buddy Drake at Penile had broken his leg badly playing a baseball game. I arrived, checked the desk, and was escorted to a room where I put on a sterile hospital gown, gloves, and a face mask. I entered Andy's room looking like something from outer space to him, I am sure. He had no idea at first who I was. Then I peeked out from under the mask for just a second and he recognized me and smiled.

He was in some pain. They had done some skin grafts. He would be well again. I prayed for him after some humorous small talk, then exited the room, took off the protective garb, and smiled and shook my head in amazement as I walked out of the hospital.

Andy healed well. His mom called on me a lot to see if I could help him. We would talk for hours about God, life, his hurts, why he got so disrespectful toward his mother at times, and just guy stuff. There was a day when he was really out of control. His mom called me. I showed up at his house, took him to a lake, sat at a picnic table with him, looked him square in the face and saw immediately I had to get his attention. He was so angry and so out of control that my usual calm talk was not going to be heard. Basically I did what is called in South Georgia, "chewing someone out." I took it to him loud, long, and continuously for about 10 minutes. He sat there in shock, and then began to cry. I had broken him.

I leaned over the table and hugged him to the side. Now I could use my calm voice. I assured him that I loved him. My intensity showed that I cared for him. I really wanted Andy to make it. I explained to him that he must stop the verbal assaults on his mother. He had a little brother that was watching him and learning from him how to act. Andy never quite got it together, though he stayed in church until the day I left Rehoboth. I made some mistakes in guiding him I am sure; some probably were glaring and huge. But I tried to show Andy the unconditional love of God. He needed that. Andy went on to marry a previously married woman, inheriting her children. I believe they had one child together also. My last contact with that family was that he was a car salesman somewhere in Atlanta. I hope Andy understands that unconditional love is still there from God . . . and a former student pastor who did the best he knew at the time.

Beth and Wade Tallant were two very special, wonderful people from a very unique family. Their parents were deaf. Both Beth and Wade were hearing. These students knew sign language. They came at life from a very different perspective. I love them to this day. I had a meal in their home one time. It was interesting to eat and carry on a conversation at the table at the same time. Beth was my translator, though her parents were also very adept at lip reading. To sign and to eat was a challenge. They did everything with lights. If the phone rang [TTY] a light flashed. If someone was at the door a light flashed. It was a very different world to me. Beth, Wade, and their parents made me feel at home in that world. There is more to share about Beth later.

Tommy was my drummer for the band. He was 20, blonde, blue-eyed, in top shape physically, with a monster sense of humor. He was not even a student in the group there. He was college-aged and helping me in the band with that ministry. During Sunday worship, the students usually sat just under the balcony on the right when you look from the platform beginning about five pews back. We were all there one morning in worship and Tommy was sitting next to me. Students have a way of spicing up a worship service that has lost its thrill. Rehoboth had some great worship, but this particular Sunday was just not up to the usual standard. We were singing the hymn, "At Calvary." The first verse is as follows:

> Years I spent in vanity and pride,
> Caring not my Lord was crucified,
> Knowing not it was for me He died,'
> On Calvary.

One of our favorite things to do was to mess with lyrics. Tommy was poised to destroy the whole student section with what came out of his mouth. It went like this:

> Years I spent in vanity and pride,
> Caring not my Lord was crucified,
> Knowing not it was for me He died,
> SO WHY CHANGE NOW!?

The whole section exploded with laughter. We had to work hard to pull ourselves back into "worship mode." Tommy seemed carefree. He had great parents, a really cool younger sister Linda in the group, and one would think Tommy had it all together.

One afternoon late there was a knock on my apartment door. I looked through the peephole and there stood Tommy. I opened the door and he got right to the point. He said that he was sorry to bother me but could he stay with me for awhile. He explained that he had a fight with his parents. He needed to cool down. They needed to cool down. It was clear that both needed some space. I pointed him to the guest bedroom, he called his parents to tell them where he was staying, and for almost a month I watched as Tommy got his head on straight again and was able to return home.

Tommy went on to become the drummer for the Billy Lord Band, a fantastic Christian praise band. In April of 2005 they performed at a celebration at Jodeco Baptist Church in Stockbridge where I served. I knew that Tommy had married and was father to two kids, a boy and a girl. I was already eating when Tommy entered the building. He spotted me and came to the table. I got up and we hugged. We did the usual small talk for guys and then as he was headed to the stage I asked, "How's your wife?" He looked ghostly and said, "She just left me. I will tell you all about it." After it was all over, we talked. Tommy was broken. The 20 year old was now a 40 something with a shattered heart. I pray for Tommy.

Jennifer. This girl was one of the drama queens in that group. She kept the boys on their toes all the time. There was constantly some big drama going on with Jennifer.

She was breaking up with a boy, about to go with a boy, sad because she was in between boys, you get the picture. I sometimes think that aliens come and snatch the brains out of middle school girls for a time. They examine the brains then when the girls turn about 16; they put the brains back in them. It seems that once a girl gets past 8th grade they begin to transform into sweet, kind, loveable people again. There was also this red-haired girl in the group that was almost a carbon copy of Jennifer in her life pattern.

DJ was a mess. He had issues. He was a 15 year-old prone to get violent with his parents when he could not have his way. He would go so far as to punch holes in the walls of the house. He was a boy headed for disaster. DJ and I would just hang out after church on the grounds and talk. For some strange reason he liked me. I liked DJ, too. I saw in him one who could do whatever he wanted if he could ever deal with the demons in his life. His parents loved him dearly. They had DJ tested and discovered that his behavior was due to a chemical imbalance in his brain, causing his synapses to misfire. This led to his violent, irrational behavior. Medication made DJ a very pleasant and fun kid to be around. The violence stopped. Then there came the day when he stopped taking the medication.

I was sound asleep in a cozy, warm bed. I was roused by the phone by my bed ringing. The alarm clock said it was after one in the morning. This could not be anything good at the other end of the line. "Hello," I said sleepily. It was DJ's voice in my ear. He very calmly announced to me that he was going to take his life and wanted to see me before he died. That got my attention. When I quizzed him as to where he was I discovered he was at the convenience store down the street from the church. Rehoboth Baptist Church had a vital prayer ministry. They even had a room on the front of the recreation center that was open 24 hours a day so that people could go there for prayer. I asked DJ to meet me in the prayer room at the church.

It was time for some fast thinking. I do not think clearly at that hour of the morning. I pulled on some clothes, slid behind the wheel of my car, breathed a prayer, turned the ignition, and drove to the church. I parked in front of the prayer room. When I opened the door there sat DJ, not looking well at all. I asked him to talk to me, to tell me why life was no longer worth living. All this teen angst began to pour out of his lips. His parents did not care about him. School was a joke. He had no friends. The list went on for a good 20 minutes. I tried to get him to see beyond the act of taking his life. Was he ready to have to tell God why he took his life into his own hands? I talked passionately about the people at the church he would leave behind and how devastated they would be. I shared with him that losing him would leave me sad and hurt. Then like a ball bat, it hit me hard. He had not been taking his medicine. I confronted him about that. He confirmed my suspicions. With all I shared with him, I could not change his mind. He was determined to end it that night. I asked him how he intended to take his life. He reached into his pocket. When he pulled out his hand, his fist unfolded to reveal some pills. I recognized them as his medication.

There were five pills. I then did what was probably a very dangerous and foolish thing in retrospect. I told him that I could not stop him from killing himself if he really was determined to do it. I locked my eyes on his and told him that I was not going to let him die alone. If he was going to die, I was going to stay with him, that no one should have to die alone. "Okay," he mumbled. The first pill went into his mouth. He looked at me defiantly, and then put the next one in his mouth. I noticed he was not swallowing them. Then he placed the third one on his tongue. By that time, I could tell he was reluctant to swallow them. Those first two pills were melting fast on his tongue by now.

He suddenly began violently spitting pills out and yelling that his tongue was on fire. I sat back and almost grinned at this scene. All along I had figured out my plan of action. If he took the pills I would simply pick up the phone in the prayer room and dial 911 and get an ambulance there. He was walking around the room by now fanning his tongue sticking out of his mouth. "I have to get something to drink," he said with urgency in his voice. I told him I would buy us both something. We got into my car and went to the convenience store up the street. I bought both of us Pepsi's. He began to cool off his tongue as I drove us back to the church.

"Let's take a walk around the ball fields," I suggested to him. As we walked, we just enjoyed the night air. As we talked I knew that DJ had turned the corner from death to life. His demeanor and talk changed. He was much calmer, thinking clearly, and had a desire to live another day. I asked him if he was ready for me to take him home. He wanted me to let him out at his house, but not to come inside in case he was confronted by his parents. All the lights were out at DJ's house. He promised to call me the next day. I sat in my car and watched him go inside his house, wave at me from the door, and close the door. I sat there for a few more minutes . . . just in case. I backed out of the driveway with a prayer of thanks to God for being in charge of a situation that I had no clue how to handle on my own.

Again, unconditional love prevailed. I loved DJ even while he was spitefully putting those pills into his mouth. God's unconditional love shown through our lives can make a tremendous difference in lives. Andy, Beth and Wade, Tommy, Jennifer, and DJ all were looking for people who would love them without question. They needed no speeches and sermons. They needed no one to judge them. They needed people to love them no matter what may happen. DJ really tested my love for him. I humbly submit that I passed his test. It was only with God's help that DJ gave me a passing grade because I was in over my head and treading water waiting for God to do something.

Student pastors, your students are testing you. This generation of students has no idea what real love is. They are abused, hurt, lonely, devoid of personality formation; proper behavior skills are practically non-existent. Yet, they are extremely bright and spiritual. They are searching. They will latch onto whatever gives them any identity, and they will run the gamut from Wicca to Goth to Christianity, often professing all at the same time. We have an opportunity to show unconditional love to this generation like no other before them. Later, I will share with you about a group of Goth students in West Hall High School and what they shared with me about this very thing of loving them. It is one of the reasons for this book.

Rehoboth Baptist Church went through the fire while I was there. As I was leaving for lunch one morning at noon, I walked to the front area where some of the secretarial offices and the pastor's office were located. The mood was somber. I saw tears in their eyes. News had broken that Pastor Buice's daughter-in-law had been brutally murdered in a park in Decatur. She and a friend she worked with had gone there for a picnic lunch, only to be accosted by a man who killed her, and wounded her friend. I got sick at my stomach. Phillip, Pastor Lester Buice's son, and his now deceased wife, and two daughters were members at Rehoboth. Leslie and Susie Buice were students in my student group. How was I going to handle this one?

As word spread throughout the day, so did the grief and pain of such a horrible event. Susie and Leslie were so beautiful. Both girls had beautiful blonde hair and fair skin just like their mother. The students were shocked and in pain. I remember how they pulled together at the family gathering at the funeral home that night. Teenagers kept showing up. The number of teens grew as the evening wore on. Leslie and Susie were seeing an outpouring of love and care like I had never seen from kids.

I do not recall who came to me that evening to ask if we could all pray for Leslie and Susie. I only remember gathering the students together in a huge circle outside the funeral home for prayer. The Buice girls joined us. I remember several teens praying and all of us weeping together. I closed the time of prayer and it was all I could do to voice a prayer because my heart was so broken for Leslie and Susie, and so blessed by the deep love and concern shown by that group of students.

The funeral and interment came and went. The weeks passed. Then my pastor, Rev. Lester Buice, did the unthinkable. The murderer had been arrested and was awaiting trial. Ironically, his last name was Wiley. Pastor Buice went to the jail and sought to lead that man who had brutally murdered his daughter-in-law to Christ. We were all stunned at his action.

That act of that pastor stands out in my mind to this day as one of the most unselfish, powerful, clearest examples of unconditional love. That he would show love and concern for the man's soul who had murdered his son's wife is incredible to me. Can God require any less from us toward those who talk us down behind our backs in our churches? When someone stands in a business meeting to question your integrity, to call you all sorts of unkind names, to question your motives and to attack you in front of the whole church, the test is on. God is watching to see how we will respond. We can respond with love that is unconditional, wishing only their best, or we can respond in anger and vindictiveness. I am sure at times you have imagined those who would undo your ministry burning in the flames of hell while you inwardly laugh with glee. God is watching. Your students are watching. The church is watching. Your character is on the line with every insult, every jab, every bit of gossip, every attack.

You and I teach our students more by what we DO than by the best Bible study we can ever teach. Students "catch" lessons from our lives. They listen to the talks and the studies, yes, but when you ask them later, it's rare that they remember what you said. They remember what you did. They remember the love.

One evening while in the middle of a home Bible study cell group my cell phone gave the incoming message alert. Luckily, I had the phone set to vibrate. I quietly flipped open the handset, pressed the button, and as I read the message I was both about to laugh and cry at once. One of the students from West Hall Middle School, now a freshman, had sent me a message. It was from a girl named Hannah. Here is how loving someone without condition can come back to you. The screen on my phone read, "Hey, Fraaaankie! We miss you like fries miss ketchup!"

CHAPTER EIGHT

THE LOVE OF MY LIFE

Unconditional love. That was Susan. If it is true that there is one woman for every man on earth, for me that woman was Susan. I will never understand fully this side of heaven why I let her go. I have never been really serious about marrying. I believe with all my heart in marriage. I believe that God has ordained marriage between one man and one woman for life. I have lived my life more like Paul and Jesus . . . single. But for a brief time God has allowed me to understand some things about relationships through a beautiful person, Susan. In her, I saw unconditional love.

In coming to Rehoboth from seminary, I really had no plans to date or to marry. It just was not a priority for me. I felt that dating a person in a church where you are a staff member can be a dangerous thing to do. I was focused on student ministry. God had given me literally hundreds of teens in this church to minister to. I was involved in planning, hospital visitation, meetings, and all the things that tend to eat away at a minister's time. Then one Sunday, there she was.

It was a Sunday morning service. A ladies' trio stepped to the microphones to sing. I could not take my eyes off this one young woman there. She had long salt and pepper hair. She was small, very petite. Less than 5 ft. tall she sang with a smile on her face that was as real as the sun that beams from the morning sky. I knew instantly the love of God was in her. She sang beautifully. Anyone who can sing well attracts me. She was no exception.

I put her out of my mind after that service. Jimmy Hicks was one of my guitarists in SKYRIDER. Jimmy is an awesome guy to this day. I love him and his wife. One night at rehearsal, I mentioned this short person to

Jimmy. Jimmy told me her name was Susan. A few days later Jimmy came to me with a grin on his face. "I have four tickets to a Russ Taff concert," he said. "Why don't you go with me and Tracy and ask Susan to come with us, too?" Tracy would become Jimmy's wife. I thought this was a great idea, so I asked Susan to go with us. My first experience with Susan was being with her at a Christian concert. I thought this was pretty nice.

Susan had a strange job. She made teeth. She worked in a dental laboratory crafting partials and plates for dental patients. We began hanging out together after church. I would have her in my home for a meal. She loved Chinese food, so we spent a lot of time talking over sweet and sour chicken, egg rolls, and wonton soup. Her parents were down-to-earth very fine people. Her mother was an excellent cook. They treated me like one of their own. She began to help in the student ministry. She loved the teenagers as much as I did. She was there for Joy Explosion every week. Never once did she complain to me about those kids getting in the way of our relationship.

Because SKYRIDER became so well-known in Atlanta it was difficult for me to go anywhere without being recognized, yelled at, and approached. I had determined that when we were away from church spending time together that I would avoid the "fans" because I felt that was our time together. I remember afternoons in Stone Mountain Park walking, sitting under the shade of a tree and talking or just being quiet together. I remember long talks at her house and at my house, as well as in our cars. It was beginning to become obvious to this hard headed guy that I really loved this person like no other. There was nothing she had not told me. I had bared my soul to her also. We still loved each other anyway.

Susan was sick. From the very beginning she had told me. She was in a constant battle with Lupus. She had already lost her spleen to the disease before I met her. It took time for her to prepare to be outdoors, whether at the park or on the beach. She would usually wear a wide-brimmed hat, which only added to her cuteness, as well as long sleeves and sunscreen. Lupus made her very sun-sensitive. The disease seemed in remission. Sometimes she would be moon-faced from the medicine she had to take. She never complained about the disease. She battled it everyday in the strength of the Lord. She was amazing.

She would travel with SKYRIDER when we would perform away from the church if she could get away. She, Tracy, and Beth, Tommy's girlfriend, eventually became back- up singers with us. We would talk on the bus, and the fellowship and laughter on the bus from David Payton, Jimmy Hicks, Tommy Worthington, John Lisenbe, Susan, Beth, and Tracy, as well as our sound tech Jim and later, Scott was wonderful as we traveled. But, all things change. As the Bryan Duncan song says, "The only thing that's certain is things are going to change."

Susan and I developed a strong bond. I brought her home for Christmas to meet my family. They fell in love with her. Christmas at my home in Sycamore has always been one of my very favorite times of life. Mom always had a huge live tree that made the whole house smell like Christmas. It was decorated beautifully. I was so pleased that mom and dad welcomed Susan the way they did. It was Christmas Eve night.

Mom and Dad retired for the evening, leaving me and Susan alone in the living room with the lighted tree. One of my warmest memories will always be the two of us cuddling by the tree just staring at it, not really saying anything. It felt good to be alive. It felt good to be there. It felt good to be with her. We eventually went our separate ways for the night. Celebrating Christmas with my family and Susan was so good. I just remember laughter and joy.

Pastor Buice suffered greatly due to the murder of his son's wife. He brought the murder up during every sermon he preached. My heart broke for him. Each worship service had this dark cloud over it. The people were waiting for him to bring it up. The deacons were so kind and patient and loving with him. Everyone loved Lester. I certainly loved him. He took me, a green and inexperienced minister, and loved me, treated me like his grandson and was nothing but kind to me. I will love him forever for that, and in heaven one day I will thank him. Alzheimer's disease took him eventually.

One Sunday after the altar call, he asked his whole family to come to the platform. They stood with him as he told the church through tears how much he loved them. He then announced his retirement effective immediately. I was shocked. He had not told his staff anything about this. As far as I know to this day, the deacons did not know he was going to do this either. Suddenly 5,000 people were without a pastor.

Things were changing. Susan and I were upset. We prayed together much about this. More and more in my mind I was close to asking her to marry me. This changed things. I had no idea what this would mean for my staff position there. The church moved swiftly and Dr. Richard Lee became the pastor of Rehoboth Baptist Church. Richard is a consummate preacher. In the pulpit he was powerful expounding the Word of God. That is Dr. Lee's great strength. I also began to see that my strong personality and his strong personality were eventually going to collide. I also knew that preachers of his ilk usually want to bring in their own staff, which is understandable.

The first staff person to go was the Minister of Music. Then one day Dr. Lee's secretary called me to set up an appointment to meet with Dr. Lee. You did not see Dr. Lee without an appointment. I had served for a year with him. I knew I was next in line for the chopping block. The day came and I met with him. Just as I expected he thanked me for serving well. He shared with me how he wanted to go in another direction with the student ministry there. He asked that I begin looking for a staff position at another church. He was very gracious. He was doing what he felt he needed to do to establish the ministries he envisioned for that church.

How was I going to tell Susan? This would change everything. My life was suddenly up for grabs in turmoil. It was a Sunday evening after church. We were in my car, parked under the awning between two of the educational buildings. It was one of the most gut-wrenching things I have ever done. I told her I was going to be leaving. I told her I did not know what to do about us. We knew we loved each other. Even in all the hurt and pain we both felt, her love was still there. Unconditional.

I had never been so confused. I had to find a place to minister. I had no time for a wedding. I had never intended to get this involved with another person anyway. My life was to minister to students. There would be no wedding. She was the love of my life, but there would be no wedding. Once I came to that decision there was no looking back, and God took care of Susan, and God was more than gracious to me.

Scott Phillips was a part of our SKYRIDER family. I had seen the way he would look at Susan. It had become obvious that there was no future for me and Susan. One day Scott came by my office to see me. I honor Scott for his class and dignity. He sat down and began to talk with me about my relationship with Susan and what my intentions might be. I told him that I did not see any way with me about to move that I could continue to pursue that relationship. He then asked me for permission to ask Susan out. He wanted to date her. What a classy man. I will never forget him. I told him he could not do any better than Susan, as much as this hurt. Scott began to date Susan and eventually married her. They had one daughter named Heather.

I moved to Rome, Georgia again. Scott and Susan had me back in their home one evening for dinner and to see their new daughter, a beautiful girl. There I was with two wonderful friends; one who could have been my wife had things worked out differently. I never looked back. I established my work in Rome and ministered there for eight years. One Thursday on my day off the phone rang. It was Jimmy. He asked me if I was sitting down. I knew this was not going to be good. I sat on the couch by the end table where the phone was in my home. Then he said, "We lost Susan last night." My immediate response was "What!?" He explained how she began to feel ill during choir rehearsal at church there at Rehoboth. They took her to the hospital and she only got worse. The Lupus was back and was attacking her blood system. She bled from most every pore as a result and died. Scott had asked Jimmy to call me and tell me and to ask if I would be one of her pallbearers. I said yes choking back tears. Jimmy did the cursory check if I was going to be all right. I lied. I was NOT going to be all right but I did not tell him that. He said he would get back to me about funeral details. I thanked him and hung up the phone.

I proceeded to fall apart. I remember falling off the couch into the floor, face down in the carpet and screaming. I was crying and screaming as if my insides would burst. I knew I was out of control. I called my church and told them to pray for me and for her family. Word spread. A few minutes passed and here they came. Some friends from the church I was serving entered my home to just be with me. I needed that and they were sensitive enough to know it. They got me through that day. They loved me unconditionally. They kept me sane. They did not say much. They were just there. They hugged me. They held me. They practiced the ministry of presence. They cried with me. They were there to just get me through it. They were the love of God and the presence of Jesus to me that day.

I have learned that when things go south for people, they do not need our words, our sermons, our questions, or our suspicions. They need US. When a kid is hurting often the best thing you can do is to just hold them. A hug goes a long way. I do not remember what my friends said to me that day. They said little. What I remember is that they were there for me. That is what your students will remember. They will remember you. They will remember your presence when they were walking through the fire.

Susan's funeral is a blur in my mind. Her body is interred across the street from the church there in a beautiful cemetery. I remember being in the limo with Jimmy, Tommy, John, and Scott. I remember the pain in my heart. I stood there graveside ready to explode. If not for Tommy's quick wit and Jimmy's quiet spirit I would have lost it. They also helped me through it.

That day I buried the love of my life. I dated a few times after our separation, but it was just never the same. Susan was the one who got away. Even now when I look at pictures of her I remember her voice, her charm, her laugh, her naiveté, and her sweet wit. I shall not forget that she showed me unconditional love. I draw from her passion for Christ this day in my own life. Her sincerity in prayer stays with me.

If you remain single in your ministry, be sure that singleness is for you. Paul describes it as a special gift that is not for everyone. The path I chose has not been easy. You must keep your life above board. Never give anyone a reason to suspect impurity. Find things to channel your time and energy into that are constructive. I found tennis and giving myself to Jesus and His church to be wonderful outlets. When a lady or a teenaged girl comes for counseling the door will either be open or there will be a big window in the door so there is no suspicion. I will never be alone with a female driving in my car. I do not go to a restaurant with a female alone. Single or married, ministers must always be on their guard and viciously protect themselves.

If you have married a wife, student pastor, cherish her. She may well be the most valuable asset to your ministry you have. She will listen when no one else will. She will lift your ministry up in prayer to the Father. She will truly be the helpmeet God intended her to be. Susan was never a detriment to my ministry. She and I prayed together often about ministry and about our relationship. She helped me guard my life from impurity. Your wife can be all that and so much more. See her as a valuable gift from God. I pray also that your spouse will show you that unconditional love of God just as Susan, the love of my life, did for me.

CHAPTER NINE

BACK TO ROME

God has a way of watching out for us even when we have no idea what He is up to. I was leaving Rehoboth. That was a done deal. My dilemma was trying to understand where I was to go. What did God have in store for me now? I sat in my office at Rehoboth one day and began wondering how to begin the search for a new place of ministry. I was so "green" and had never had to deal with finding a new place to serve God. I felt totally unprepared for this move. I knew I wanted to leave quickly. There was no need to linger any longer than I had to.

I picked up the phone and called Second Avenue Baptist Church just to let them know I was looking around and ask them to let anyone know that may be looking for a student pastor. It was no time when my phone rang and on the other end of the line was Carlton Keith. Carlton was a member of Second Avenue Baptist Church. He was also chairman of the search committee looking for a student pastor for that church. He asked me if I would be interested in talking with them about returning to Second Avenue.

For a moment, I sat there stunned. This I had never even thought possible. Most people never get a second chance. But it was not long before the deal was done and I was packing my things, saying goodbye to the students at Rehoboth, and driving to Rome, Georgia after almost 7 years. A familiar church waited with a new pastor, new students, many who were little babies almost my first time there. I stepped out on faith and the next eight years would be filled with some awesome kids, awesome experiences, and some painful things as well.

I set out to build the best ministry to students in Floyd County. I began looking for musicians. I wanted to get a weekly worship for teens started. As

I asked people about musicians, one name kept coming up: Chris Hodges. I went to his home to visit him, get to know him and to ask him to be my drummer. Chris proved to be a most gifted musician. In Chris, I got more than I ever imagined I would. He sang. He was a solid drummer. He was a writer, and he could play guitar. Chris is one of the most gifted musicians I have ever had the privilege to walk on stage with. He knew Terry West, a bass player. I could definitely handle the keyboards and invested in a rack of keyboards anchored by a Yamaha DX7 as the master keyboard driving a Roland JX8P through the midi system, a powerful combination. We went through several guitarists until Jimmy Hicks committed to drive to Rome for Tuesday rehearsal and Thursday meetings and be our guitarist. He was my guitarist in SKYRIDER. Jimmy got us off to a very fine start in Rome. Eventually, the driving became a bit much for Jimmy. He had married and his wife was first priority. Enter Scotty Davis. Scotty was quiet, had a distinct southern rock flavor to his playing that I love and was important for us as a band. Yet he was versatile enough to play "new wave" and "blues" and other styles we used. The band DMZ was formed. The four of us in Rome would make local history and reach literally hundreds of teenagers.

The students there were upper middle class kids who had most everything they wanted. There were sons and daughters of doctors and accountants and lawyers and college professors. Rusty Day stood out to me from the very beginning of my ministry there. He was a strawberry blonde jock, quiet, kind, and cute. Rusty was the one who always spent time with the little kids in the church loving on them. If we were on a mission trip, he was the same way. He was very good with little children, very patient and very loving and kind to them.

I had Rusty pegged as a future student pastor. He would be great at it, I thought. I was not far off in my assertion. Rusty became a Middle School teacher and coach.

Lori Bennett was a "mess" growing up. I loved her. She kept all the boys on their toes. Bobby Keith did not have a prayer when she was around. She kept Rusty on his guard, too. Lori had a huge heart as a teen. I remember the day that became clear. Lori called me at the church and asked if she could bring a friend by to talk with me who needed help. She arrived with a friend who was broken, shattered, confused, and in need of great hope.

Through tears this young lady shared with me how she had been technically "raped" at a party. She had too much to drink, passed out, and one of the boys at the party took advantage of her sexually at the party in front of the others there. I cannot describe the humiliation and shame that was pouring out of that precious girl. It took her eons to tell her story because there were times all she could do was to sit and cry. When she would get herself under control again she would share the next chapter in this ugly event.

What do you say to a young lady feeling so ashamed and so abused? Girls in her position need to know first and foremost, I believe, that they are still loved and still are valuable and have worth. I told her that it took courage to share such a painful story. I shared with her that God still loves her and there is forgiveness in Him for what had happened. I knew she was feeling guilt and shame. It was not my job to reinforce that. My role was to point her to the hope that is in Jesus through His sacrifice. I pointed her to forgiveness.

On a more practical level, I also shared with her that she should tell her parents and be tested for pregnancy and disease, if for no other reason than her peace of mind. And if she was pregnant it was not the end of the world. That child could be adopted, raised by her parents, or even herself under the right conditions. She left the office that day with hope and a practical plan all because of Lori Bennett caring enough to get a hurting friend some help. Lori and I showed her unconditional love that day. It made the difference in her life.

Ben Hansard was the middle son of three boys. Ben had a sharp sense of humor and loved a good time. He was a kidder. Ben was faithful, there for everything at church. I got wind one day that Ben's interests had turned to boxing. He wanted to be a professional boxer and as an older teen now, he got involved with the local boxing scene there in Rome. His mother was appalled. His father was not fond of the idea either, but supported Ben's ambition. I attended one of Ben's boxing matches with his dad. His mom would not come to the matches because she could not watch her son get the stuffing beaten out of him. And that is exactly what happened that night. Ben got his clock cleaned!

Ben continued on that path with all that goes along with that lifestyle. When I eventually left Second Avenue for Toccoa I lost touch with Ben . . . for awhile. Years later his father, Larry, called me. Larry wanted me to know that Ben had surrendered to preach and was studying for ministry. The last I heard from Ben was that he was pursuing that call. I bet the deacons do not mess with him for fear of getting beaten up! I walked with Ben into his life. I showed him love even when he was drifting after being so faithful. Perhaps in some small way God used that to get Ben focused on His call on Ben's life.

I want you to meet Steven. Steven is further proof that when you love someone unconditionally, warts and all, they will "get it" and will return that love in ways you never imagined. Steven showed up for everything. But he never came inside. On Sunday nights he was there. On Thursdays at DMZ, he was there. Rarely if ever would he leave his truck and come inside. The meetings would dismiss and all the teens would be all over the lawn talking and being teens, and Steven would sit in his truck alone.

I would always go over to his truck and strike up a conversation with him. We would talk about whatever. I knew that Steven had a drug problem. He knew that I knew. Steven was testing me and the group to see if anyone cared. I never really saw a change in Steven, but I always loved him. Occasionally he would come inside on Thursday's to hear the band, but never related to the other students. He was the "stoner loner" in the group.

It was six years after I had left Second Avenue. I had come on staff at Poplar Springs Baptist Church as their Minister of Music and Student Pastor. The secretary rang my office to transfer a call. It was Steven. He was calling me to tell me he was marrying and he asked me to perform the ceremony. I do not do weddings without at least three counseling sessions with the bride and groom. I asked him how we were going to accomplish that distance between Rome and Gainesville, Georgia. He said they were willing to drive the distance for counseling. It was apparent that he was committed to me being the one to perform the wedding ceremony.

In that first session with Steve and his bride, I asked him why he chose me to perform the wedding when the pastor at Second Avenue would have gladly done that and was quite a fine man. Steven got really quiet for a minute, and then he looked up at me. What he shared drew tears from my eyes right there on the spot.

He quietly said, "Frankie, you were the only person when I was a kid who knew I was smoking pot and had problems, yet you had a way of always jumping across that fence and coming to me when I would show up and just sit in my truck." What he was saying is that I loved him regardless of his problems and never judged him because of them. He sensed God's love from me to him. I humbly began to weep and very softly and broken I managed to get out "thank you." It was a further joy to know that Steven was clean and sober and beginning to grow as a young Christian.

You never fully understand the impact the simple act of having a conversation with a stoner kid can have on their life. Unconditional love does not mean you accept a student's behavior if it's sinful. It means that you love them in spite of that. Somehow in your love they will sense you want the best for them. On some level they begin to understand that you don't like their sin but you do love THEM anyway and you would never want any harm to come to them. A conversation by a truck, sitting with the Goths at a high school, or whatever act of love you perform God honors and it bears fruit. Steven is a trophy to me and God's confirmation that eight years of ministry there was not wasted.

This kid was angry. Jacob was 13. He came to us at Second Avenue from Oklahoma. His family attended Second Avenue Baptist Church because they lived one block away from the church. Jacob did not want to be in Rome and he proceeded to let everyone know it. He started smoking. His language was less than pristine. One day he showed up at church with a multi-colored Mohawk haircut, shaved on the sides and back and straight up into the air in the middle like a rooster's cone! His parents were deeply concerned, and frankly, so was I. This is the first student I had ever met so blatantly in rebellion over something. But God called me to love Jacob or he would not have put Jacob across my path.

Jacob loved DMZ and wanted to learn to play guitar, which I am able to this day to teach. His mother approached me about teaching him. It was in the course of those lessons that I built a friendship and an understanding of Jacob I had never had before. Underneath the haircut, the cigarettes, and the potty mouth was a fragile 13 year old boy who was really hurting. I would teach him guitar. At the end of each lesson I would draw him out to talk and a 30 minute lesson would turn into 40 or 50 minutes as he opened up to share his feelings.

I discovered that Jacob was angry because he did not want to leave Oklahoma. He was missing his friends there, he had made no friends in Rome, and he did not want to be in Rome. He was upset with his parents because they made him move. I did a lot of listening for a few weeks. Eventually I began so share my understanding of his anger. I was also quietly asking some of the boys in the group at church to pay him attention and build a friendship with him. I shared with his parents what I had learned about his behavior. They took some steps to reassure Jacob and help him. We literally loved the anger and hatred out of that boy. It was not too long that I noticed he had stopped smoking. His hair grew out and returned to "normal." His language was becoming less and less offensive. Jacob became one of the most loving kids in that group. Why? His student pastor loved him enough to hang with him through all the weirdness. Also, a group of teens got wise and began to love him too and pay him attention. God changed Jacob's life because of unconditional love.

There are students that crossed my path at Second Avenue that I must mention because they were faithful, solid, great kids who have grown up and have become successful as adults. Matt and his sister Elizabeth Bowen were tremendous teenagers. There was Ande Barden, the pastor's daughter who was extremely bright and forceful as a teen. She is successful as a business woman today. Chad Sharp was just that . . . sharp. He was a cute jock who has successfully grown into adulthood. I also remember Rich Foldes, Matt Stahl, Don Chambers, Brett, Mike and Meleitha Ingle, and Benny Corntassel. There was Daniel Pinson, always the mouth because of his size. He had to bully people verbally because he was small and knew everyone else could beat him up. Daniel is now married and doing well when I last checked on him. Karen and Jan Jones were super young ladies who always carried themselves in a Godly way. There are too many people I met down through my eight years at Second Avenue to name them all and give them adequate treatment here.

DMZ, the meeting, grew weekly. DMZ, the band, would perform a set, followed by Bible study, usually evangelistic, and an altar call. Many students came to Christ in that meeting. I spent many nights in the lounge behind the stage area of the fellowship hall praying with kids coming to Jesus, as did the other members of the band. The meeting eventually packed out the fellowship hall. God did an unusual thing during the years that meeting ran.

We wanted to do something to impact the community through the band. We took a leap of faith, rented the De Soto theater downtown, and began practicing and publicizing a New Year's Eve Jam. This was an old movie theater that had been converted into a rather nice place for live theater. The stage was great. The acoustics were really fine. For two years in a row we packed that theater out as over 500 kids came each year for the concert. In 1985 on New Year's Eve the place sold out. SKYRIDER was still together and came to be on the ticket with us. For three hours we rocked the house. DMZ played as tightly as any live band I have ever heard. The crowd was electric the whole evening, and students came to Christ. I will never forget that.

DMZ put out two projects, "Society's Slave" and "Reason for Tears." We did a small tour up to Myrtle Beach, S.C. one summer. That was a blast. We played in the pavilion by the beach that was there before a hurricane took it all away. The crowds were small, but we had so much fun hanging out with kids on the beach and just being together. Then it happened.

I knew Rob Fricks when he was a kid. The day he called me as an adult I thought he had to be pulling a joke on me because Rob was like that, a prankster. Rob was running a small booking agency there in Rome. What he asked me had to be a joke. "Would you guys in DMZ like to open for Stryper?" he asked. I asked him if this was a sick joke. Stryper was the biggest heavy metal Christian band at the time and had even crossed over and MTV was playing one of their videos. Rob was not kidding. He had booked them to come to Rome in between shows in Atlanta and South Carolina. They needed an opening act and we were the best band in town. Actually we were better known in Rome than was Stryper. Rob knew this and our name on the ticket would help draw people. When I approached the rest of the guys about this, they thought I was joking. Once I assured them I was not, they jumped at the idea.

At the Rome City Auditorium we opened for Stryper. These guys were so nice to us. They were living offstage and backstage what they were singing about onstage. Michael Sweet is one of the most intelligent, thoughtful musicians I have met. He and I were talking at one point that evening about music. They were on the "Soldiers Under Command" tour at the time because that album had taken off and had huge success. We were talking about how some well-meaning Christians really condemn the kind of music they and us were doing. They just don't get it. When I expressed that, Michael looked at me and grinned, and then he said, "If you think people are offended now by what we are doing, just wait until our next project is released. They are really going to go ballistic." I asked him what it was going to be. He said simply, "To Hell with the Devil." I am thankful that I had the experience of performing on the same stage with those guys. They were real. They were genuine. For a time after their success, they wandered in the wilderness in a bad place. It is my understanding that they are true to their Christian beliefs again today. I wish Michael, Robert, Tim, and Oz the very best blessings of God.

DMZ was not always well-accepted by the Christians in Rome. We decided that we wanted to do a show in the beer garden at Schroeder's New Deli downtown. We would do it early before the hardcore drinkers got there. We would not compromise the message. We would stay true and be a witness in a place that needed the gospel. Shannon Schroeder was very accepting of the idea and we did the show.

A few days later a letter arrived on my desk. It was from a well-meaning but very narrow-minded pastor in the community. The letter was highly critical of us. It was harsh, rude, judgmental, and way off-base. I did not sense any love emanating from those pages. To him, we were wolves in sheep's clothing, using the devil's music and claiming to use it for God. He wanted to know how we could call ourselves Christians and play in such a place as a beer garden. We were fake Christians. We were doing the devil's work.

I could not resist this one. I replied to his letter. As clearly but as lovingly as I could I challenged him on every point. First, if you are going to catch fish, you have to use the right bait. We are simply fishing for souls of students who like that music to "hook" them to hear the gospel. I also asked him to recall that Jesus hung out with winebibbers and people of low reputation. We were just being like Jesus. I also challenged him at the point of our salvation. He had never met us. He did not know us. How could he pass judgment on us and our motives and whether we were Christians or not when he had never taken the time to meet with us and get to know us first? I then asked him to consider that his time might be better spent getting out there where the sinners are and sharing Jesus with them instead of writing hostile letters from the shadows to people he did not even know and standing in judgment of them. I never heard from that guy again.

After three years of performing weekly, two fine recording projects, opening for a major act, packing out a theater, and rocking Myrtle Beach, we were tired. Chris was in love. I had sensed our interests beginning to go in other directions. Chris' mother and father had traveled with us and his dad had been our sound technician. Both parents had been wonderful band parents to us. He was faithful and did as good a job as any sound tech I have ever seen. But it was "time to go." DMZ would be no more. God had used us to reach more students than I had ever imagined possible. We had made some incredible music. In the years that followed the break-up I tried some other bands, but none of the caliber of DMZ.

The first mission trip I ever did with students was from Second Avenue Baptist Church. Our students went to Gatlinburg, Tennessee one summer and worked in the campgrounds under the leadership of Bill and Cindy Black, resort missionaries to Gatlinburg. There were six teams of students working in six different campgrounds during the day. I floated among the campgrounds daily to be sure everything was on target. The student pastor becomes whatever he needs to be to encourage students during such difficult work. A student pastor wants the experience to be positive for the group. They should return home knowing that God used them, they were successful, and with the expectation of experiencing another mission endeavor as soon as possible.

To achieve those goals one builds in several things. I always look for the area where students may be unsure of what to do, or feeling overwhelmed at a task. I was in a campground one morning and saw Heather Schwettman at a table totally freaking out and on the verge of tears. I quietly slid next to her to discover that she had more children in day camp than she had bunny ears for a craft they would make later that day. Heather's heart was incredible. She did not want to let any of the children down. She was upset because some of the kids would not have bunny ears. "Let's see what we have," I reassuringly said to her. I dove into the "emergency box" each team had. There was a huge stack of paper plates. I asked her if the children would mind if some of the bunnies had white ears instead of pink ears. She began to understand and a smile broke out on her face. With scissors in hand Heather and I cut out white bunny ears from some of those paper plates so the children could all carry a bunny rabbit they had made back to their campsite to give to their parents. Heather felt great the rest of the day because she was part of the solution to a problem that made the kid's day!

I also build in "play time" or "down time" so the students can decompress. The midway point of a mission trip can be especially tense. I seek to build in a day that is "different" for students on the day that falls half-way through a mission project. It may be a sight-seeing trip that the students are completely unaware of until they are on the way. It may be a special meal, or a special worship experience. I have extended free time or planned an evening where nothing happens except the students are together relaxing, bonding, and making memories.

Claudia and Elissa were awesome with the little children. One thing I caution my students about is the attachment they will feel with children they work with on a mission trip, whether in Gatlinburg, Tennessee or Kingston, Jamaica. I remember the tears they shed when a little blonde, green-eyed boy with freckles looked over his dad's shoulder and with a wave and "bye" was gone because his vacation was over that day. Harold Hilliard and Jim Kelly, Matt Bowen, Adam Turner, and the others on that mission trip rose to every challenge. Adam left for the mission trip immature and with an attitude. Adam was an extremely smart young teen. He is one of those kids that, despite their horrendous attitudes at times, you cannot help but love. I brought Adam home a changed young man from that mission trip. He transformed that week. From my experience with Adam and so many others like him, I am convinced of several things concerning mission experiences for teenagers.

I know that there was a paradigm shift in 80's concerning the "call" to missions. When I was a teenager you went down the aisle in a church on Sunday and told your church that you had been called to missions. God sometimes still works that way. He is God. He can do whatever He wants to do and needs to do. The shift has been away from that "walking the aisle" experience. I have seen students hear the voice of God to them for missions while they are out on a mission trip actually already DOING missions and tell the trip leader or the student pastor or some adult while on the trip.

I am also convinced that if you want your students to grow exponentially in their walk with Jesus at least one major mission project a year is in order. Adam grew spiritually more in one week than he had grown in a full year while in Gatlinburg. I find myself growing in my walk faster than during a "normal" week of ministry.

A mission trip focuses a teenager on the mission, and forces them out of their comfort zones to a place where they must rely on the Spirit of God. In planning sessions I always seek to prepare students for that very thing. I tell them that we will plan everything down to the last detail and be prepared so that everything runs smoothly, and that when we arrive on the mission field we will throw all those plans out the window because mission trips become nothing like you have planned and envisioned. A later chapter will deal more with mission trips.

Howard Ingle was one of the deacons at Second Avenue. Howard had always been one of my favorite people. When I returned to Second Avenue to begin the second wave of ministry there, one morning he and I were on the front side entrance talking. I was feeling overwhelmed that I actually had been re-called to that place to serve again. I very seriously said to him, "I feel so honored and blessed to be able to serve here a second time." Without cracking a smile, Howard wryly replied, "We brought you back here to clean up the mess you left the first time."

Now, eight years from that new beginning, I had helped that church through a pastoral change that took a long time. Other staff was part-time with other jobs. The interim pastor was only there Wednesdays and Sundays. It fell to me to visit the hospitals and tend to that great flock. They found a new pastor, a good one in Dr. Ken Ross. Ken and I related well. But, I was getting old in the tooth now having been there for eight years. Some people even began saying some very unkind and mean-spirited things concerning me and the ministry there. I am amazed at how un-Christian Christians can be at times. The tongue is powerful. I pray for the day when Christians will use that power to tell people about Jesus instead of attack other Christians and tear down people's lives.

God was clear with me. This ministry is finished. Looking back I had nothing to be ashamed of. My conscience was clear. I had loved those people dearly. I had built a student ministry that was on the cutting edge of student work and did not even realize it. God had used me in so many ways to reach students for Christ. I think of Dan Starnes and Steven Lackey. Out of that group have come preachers and missionaries. The Ben Hansards and the Bobby Newmans will never be forgotten.

I left Second Avenue Baptist Church with no place to go. After eight years God knew I needed something different. I needed a vacation. I was burned out, hurt, broken, and tired. It was time for a wilderness experience. I sold my house, put all my belongings in storage, got into my car, stopped at the Floyd County line, got out of my car, took my shoes off, and shook the dust off my feet, never to return again without an invitation. I sat down behind the wheel, breathed a prayer asking God to help me, then I drove south into a whole new time of life for the next six months.

Bobby Keith handed me a card at my going-away party. Bobby was a great kid. His good looks kept the girls panting. He was a jock, but underneath the good looks and the athleticism was a very tender heart. I close this chapter sharing with you a bit of what was in that card that he had written. He shared all the good times and what I had meant to his life. He closed the note with this, which I have read time and again: "And now I am going to say something that I have never said to another man: I love you."

CHAPTER TEN

A MINISTRY OF A DIFFERENT KIND

As I headed south for home on that day, my mind replayed in vivid detail all the burnout, depression, pain, and sadness I had felt during my last days in Rome.

There was a period when I fell into deep depression. I remember that at one point I kept the house dark mostly and literally sat on the couch for what seems to be almost three days staring at nothing. I had quietly sought professional Christian counseling. Through that, I realized clearly that there were some very personal things I had to walk away from. I got a very clear picture of who I really was in Christ and it was nothing like what I perceived myself to be. When I left Rome, I left a lot of things behind. The counseling was needed and helpful, even when the pressures and personal pain I had bottled up came again to undo me.

The break-up with Susan, then her death, the move to Rome, the incredible pace I had kept with ministry and DMZ, added to seeking to help hold that church together, and the loss of my grandmother who I adored all conspired to make me unable to effectively minister. I needed a break. I had made some mistakes out of all this depression. I needed something totally different. My passion was and is to this day reaching students, loving teenagers. That is God's call on my life. But I had not taken care of ME. I had lost my zeal, my passion, and I did not care anymore. God knew I needed a break from "church."

I never strayed from my faith in Jesus Christ. If not for His grace and mercy to me during those days of personal darkness, I quite possibly would have taken my life. I remember sitting on that couch during those days of depression and just wanting my life to be over. One man made a difference. Dr. Ken Ross, my pastor at the time, dropped by to see me. He had no agenda. He simply came to say in his own way that he cared. He knew what was wrong with me. He stood with me. I honor him for that. It was his visit that, in the midst of all the storms in my soul, helped pull me out of this deep chasm I had fallen into.

The farther I drove from Rome the more relaxed I felt. I was headed home to stay with my parents for awhile. I arrived to hugs, handshakes, and kisses. Mothers have a sixth sense. It did not take my mother long to zero in on my psyche. She could see the depression and pain. In her very special way she gently and lovingly lit a fire under me. She knew my passion for kids. She also knew that if I sat around the house that I would not get any better. I needed something fresh, different, but that involved teenagers. I also knew that I needed income, because I still had bills to pay, mainly a car payment monthly. She suggested that I become a substitute teacher at Turner County Middle School until God opened a door for me to get back into ministry in a church.

I took the training and went through the background checks. It was not too long before that school was using me almost on a daily basis. God was providing my need. In the halls of that school I was reminded that ministry is sometimes best done outside the church walls.

My first morning as a substitute teacher sent a message to the students that I was not to be messed with. My presence there also eventually showed teachers who had given up on certain students that they were missing it completely. As I walked down the hall with the assistant principal toward the class I was to teach I heard the students loud and clear. Their teacher had not arrived and it had just hit them that there would be a sub in that classroom. Party time! But I had a plan. I was going to take that classroom by force.

I walked through the door, grabbed the door and slammed it just hard enough to make a loud noise as it shut behind me. The room went quiet immediately and every head snapped to look in surprise at the door. I instantly began talking with authority in my voice as I moved toward the board to write down who I was and what I expected. "Good Morning! My name is Mr. Wiley and I will be teaching you today. I expect that you listen, follow instructions and do the assigned work, and that you do not talk without permission. Now, I am going to take roll."

Not one smart remark was made as those 12 year-olds responded to the roll call. I then gave them their work for the hour, and proceeded to walk the rows of desks in that room to be sure the students were working on the assignment, to let them know they were being watched, and to be available for questions regarding the assignment. The first hour passed without incident. The day was good. But I came home around 3:30 exhausted. The energy of Middle School kids is incredible. The volume levels they can reach in the cafeteria and on the playground is beyond that of a jet taking off. My deep respect and prayers go to Middle School teachers to this day for daily walking into that and teaching and loving those students, as loud and obnoxious as they can be at times.

One day I was subbing for the band teacher for one period. He had to be away during my free period that day and Mr. Baxter, the principal, asked me to sit with that class. There are occasions when students will test you. It is not always that they do not understand where the lines of behavior are drawn. Sometimes they just have to see if you really meant what you said regarding behavior. Students often test a sub just to see what they are made of. I have a term of endearment I use to describe middle school boys, especially those who have to test you and push you. I call them "goat heads." Two goat heads decided they wanted to break out in a fight in the band room. The instant they started I never flinched. I simply reached for the intercom button and said, "Mr. Baxter, can you please come to the band room. It seems two boys here want to fight." From the floor in a pile, the two boys looked up at me stunned and immediately stopped fighting and began straightening the chairs they had knocked over. Mr. Baxter walked in and removed the two boys from the classroom. I looked at the rest of the class and with steely blue eyes that meant business, pointed to the floor and said, "Would anyone else like to try that?" I waited for five seconds. "I didn't think so!" I sternly said. Word spread through school that day that you do not want to mess with Mr. Wiley.

The other teachers had warned me about Willy. He was trouble. I should keep an eye on him. He was a constant discipline problem in their classes. I inherited Willy for two weeks or more when his 8th grade teacher broke her leg practicing for the Student-Faculty Basketball game. His name was Willy McCoy. Willy was African-American. His mother was a known crack addict in town. It was a horrible situation he had to grow up in. I knew God had put Willy in my path for a reason. Math was difficult for Willy. I had Willy for one hour each day in math class. Willy was in for some changes.

I would walk that class room daily helping students with math problems. Willy would invariably call my name because he did not understand something. There were times when I had to go over the solution to a math problem several times before he understood how I arrived at the answer. After a few days he asked me if he could clean the board and the erasers. I was already keeping Willy so busy with math he did not have time to show out in class. Now, he was asking to do something for me. Here was my chance.

I made a deal with Willy. He could clean the board and the erasers each day the last 10 minutes of class only if he had all of his work done and had been good. Willy never missed a day of cleaning the board and the erasers. I was talking to a teacher one day in the hallway. In the flow of things Willy would leave my math class and go to her class. She looked at me seriously that day and asked me, "What have you done to Willy?" I asked her what she meant by that statement. She shared with me that since I had taken over the class, she has noticed that Willy is hardly a discipline problem anymore when he arrives in her class. I was just doing what I know to do. Willy needed attention. He had no father. He needed male attention. He needed authority. He needed someone to love him and show it by helping him and trusting him with some things. Willy never let me down. I am not sure what happened to Willy. I have lost touch with him. I know this. If for no other reason, God put me in that Middle School to show an undisciplined, hardened, and hurting 13 year-old kid that there is real love in the world. There were no conditions on my love for Willy. I simply loved him and let God's love show itself in me to him.

I was healing. My mind was feeling clear. I was feeling refreshed. I saw hope for my future again. In God's timing, the phone rang one evening at my parents' home. It was Bruce Adams calling. He was from Tom's Creek Baptist Church in Martin, Georgia, just outside of Toccoa. They were looking at my resume and had checked my references and talked with people at previous churches I had served and they wanted to meet with me about a position in their church. This would be a ministry I had never done before, both youth and worship. I was wide-eyed as it dawned on me that perhaps God, after a period of much needed "downtime" from church ministry, was about to move me back into the church with expanded territory and bigger responsibilities. What a wise, on-time God we serve!

I drove to Toccoa, praying all the way. I was following the directions they gave me to get to Tom's Creek Baptist Church. Toward Martin I found that I was driving through country. There was only me, the road, and chicken houses, and cattle. I was thinking that surely there is a church somewhere out here. I rounded a bend in the country two lane road and there it was! The church looked like a train. The sanctuary was the large engine and the two educational buildings directly behind it connected by sheltered walkways were the cars. There was a gym at the rear of the back parking lot. The pastorium and fellowship hall sat off to the left of the sanctuary. Bruce and one other man met me there.

The meeting went well. The vote was coming. Meanwhile, I remained at home waiting for their call.

Ministers, hear me. Do a better job of balancing your ministry with time for yourself, and if you are married, with time for your family. My reckless abandon to ministry and making music and holding a church together that was without a pastor, plus not dealing well with parting from Susan, then her death, plus my grandmother's death was a huge failure in my life. It brought a sad end to a vibrant, cutting-edge ministry. I was no good to Second Avenue Baptist Church or to anyone. God's loving intervention through that church's seeing there was nothing more I could do effectively there, a pastor's quiet love and care for me, and the prayers of people who loved me were my saving grace.

I do not wish for you a couch of depression and hurt. I had to learn to balance my life the hard way. I had to learn not to take myself too seriously through a lot of personal pain. I am convinced now that I am not Superman after all. It took dark days on a couch with no vision of a future to bring me to a place where God could break me, remold me, and make me more effective than I had ever been.

If you are hurting, minister, tell someone. Do not keep it inside thinking that people will think you are unfit as a minister if they know. We are all human, with feet of clay. We need one another. There may be those who will decide that God has told them you are unfit to minister because you have a problem. Do not let judgmental people deter you from doing what is right. God still had plans for me. God has plans for you, too. God will never turn His back on his children. Confiding in Dr. Ross was the best thing I ever did. It opened the door for God's healing to begin.

I still miss Susan deeply to this day. My grandmother Wiley is very much a part of who I am now. I have learned that truly there is no condemnation for those who are in Christ Jesus, no matter what people say. The things I learned making music is now paying dividends as God has shown me some exciting ways to use it without so much pressure. In retrospect I have learned valuable life lessons from walking through churches without pastors. God has shown me how to use those lessons to be a more effective minister. I gained insights into human nature I had never seen before.

On the other side of the pain, God has proven His Word in Romans 8:28.

> "For we know that all things work together for good to them that love the Lord, to those who are called according to His purpose."

CHAPTER ELEVEN

FACING DOWN RACISM

And so it was that Tom's Creek Baptist Church invited me to join them in ministry. Clack Stubbs was pastor then. He and his wife Hazel are wonderful people.

They took me right in and treated me like a son. I learned much from Clack. He is a no-nonsense man of God who preaches hard and loves people intensely. You always know where you stand with him.

One of the best things he did for me was to challenge me to more Scripture memory. He made it fun. We always met on Mondays. During the course of our planning and praying we both chose a Scripture to memorize during the week. We would meet again on Friday and quote our selected Scriptures to one another. This was fruitful in many ways. It held both of us accountable. It kept me in the Word reading and studying. It greatly increased my memorized portions of Scripture. Clack and his wife continue this day to be friends of mine. It was a joy to serve with such a real man of God again.

The students were your typical country mountain kids. They were rough around the edges. Some dipped. Some smoked. The boys were sexually aggressive. Their language was often so vile that grass died where they would spit. It was going to be a rewarding ministry, though some tough decisions lay ahead. The girls were sweet and kind, and were the strength that kept the boys in line. There was a division in the group that actually carried over into the whole congregation.

I first realized this schism in talking to a deacon not long after beginning the work there. Winfred Addison was one of the older men of the church. I love him dearly to this day, him and his wife. Winfred was "old school" though. One day in the course of conversation he asked me where I was living. I told him that I was living in Toccoa, about seven miles from the church situated in Martin. He asked me why I was living there and not out near the church. My reply was that it was closer to the grocery store, restaurants, the post office and things I needed to be near. He looked at me slyly, and then with a grunt said, "I guess that's all right. Just don't bring any of that out here."

In the student group that remark manifested itself this way. I had really two student groups on my hands. There were those local students who lived very near the church, kids like Eddie and Bobby, Rusty and Justin, the Waters girls, and Blake. There were other teens that lived in town. I began to observe that the local teens were isolating the "city kids." The weekly student worship meeting I established there began to help bridge that gap, but there always remained some tension between the two.

I also began to gain insights into mountain people. Mountain people are a close- knit, clannish group of people. This is not a criticism. This is just the way they live life. They are very suspicious of anyone who comes in from the outside. The local people are not very fond of Toccoa Falls College being there because that was established by Northerners. I too was an outsider and was being watched. My pastor told me once he was really surprised at how quickly they took me into the life of the church. Thus, the stage was set for some great yet challenging days. I set about the business of creating the most excellent worship possible with what we had, and to raise the bar on student ministry to a whole new level.

The musicians were really good. Karen and Janet anchored the piano and organ. There were some great voices in the choir which really began to grow and sound better and better. There were some high moments of worship there. One Easter, I decided to close the service with the choir backing me singing "I Bowed on My Knees and Cried Holy." This was the original Brooklyn Tabernacle arrangement done with Michael English. We launched into the song and all heaven broke loose. I was getting emotional. The choir was beginning to weep. People in the congregation began lifting hands and crying. On the last note and cut-off the sanctuary roared with applause and people weeping and shouting. We had all experienced God. From that day forward that song became branded as my trademark vocal.

How do you minister to a kid like Eddie? Eddie was cunning. He was an extremely cute young boy with dimples, freckles, black hair, and hazel eyes. He was little in stature yet broad shouldered and well built. He had a friendly disposition that belied the fact that there was a little of the devil himself inside Eddie. Eddie lived in a trailer with his mother and step-dad. His step-father, Jim, was good to Eddie and was raising him like his own. Eddie's coming to be where he was is a complicated family tree. I spent much time in their home. Most visits were pleasant, but sometimes the visits were not comfortable, for every now and then, Eddie would do something stupid. Eddie enjoyed coming to my home every now and then. God had put Eddie in my path for a reason. Through Eddie I learned that you cannot always make a popular decision. Sometimes, for a teen's own welfare, you have to get really tough.

It was summer. Plans were laid for a week-long retreat in Panama City for our students. Eddie was one of the first ones to pay his deposit and sign up. I was quietly thanking God that he was going, that maybe the retreat would put him in a position to listen to God. At the same time I was asking God for strength to deal with his energy and his deviousness. Several weeks before the retreat, the church sponsored Vacation Bible School for the children of the church and community. Our teens worked in different roles that week in the school. Eddie was one of them. His friend Chris was also there.

One afternoon after VBS the pastor came to me and asked me to go look at a classroom where the children had met that morning. When I walked through the door I was immediately angry. My stomach sank. What lay before me was total chaos. Things were scattered everywhere. The crafts the children had made were broken. Glitter and glue were just strewn everywhere. Some chairs were turned over. The classroom had been totally trashed. Clack asked me if I had any idea how that happened. We quickly ran down the list of students helping with VBS. In the midst of that I remembered that Eddie had not gone directly home, but had hung out at the church.

Through talking with some students and thinking it through, it became clear that Eddie was the one responsible for the destruction. I then met with the deacons to get their backing and approval for what the pastor and I were about to do. When I had confronted Eddie he all but admitted doing it. I had decided that since he was the vandal, that there was no way he could last the whole week away from the church and out of state on a retreat. With the deacons' approval, the pastor and I went just up the road to the trailer, cash in hand with bad news. We told his mom and his step-dad in no uncertain terms what Eddie had done, and the penalty was that he could not go to Panama City with the students and we were refunding his money. His mom understood, but Jim did not so understand. He pitched one unholy fit. We stood our ground. Eddie stayed home. He learned a lesson. In the process of his learning, I also learned that you do the right thing, not the thing to appease parents and kids so they like you. Eddie and I remained friends. I had some work to do to rebuild the relationship with his family, and that happened. To this day, I have a very warm and loving place in my heart for that kid. You can love a kid regardless of what they do. You are not required to love what they do but you are required to love them. Sometimes the most loving thing you can do for an out-of-control kid is the hardest thing to do. But it needs to be done. You could be a lifeline for a kid in the process.

One Sunday the South's joined Tom's Creek. Sherry and Devin were young and a very attractive couple. Two boys were in tow with them. The younger of the two, Britt, was about 10. Rusty was 13. These boys were Sherry's children by a previous marriage. One look at Rusty and you could see pain and hurt in him. The divorce had been hard for him. Rusty was quiet and laid back, a thoughtful young guy. Britt was a typical big-mouthed 10 year-old with big eyes and a cocky attitude. I loved these boys at first sight. Devin was in law enforcement. Devin was also trying to be a good step-father to those boys. The boys were resistant to say the least.

Knowing I played guitar, Rusty's mom approached me one day and asked if I would teach him guitar. Rusty had become interested in learning to play. I took him on as a student and that relationship has paid dividends down through the years for Rusty and for me, as well as for Britt. Rusty was a great student. He learned quickly. He practiced hard. When I raised the standard on him he always rose to the occasion. Those times became healing for Rusty.

He began to talk to me some about his family. I would listen. I would encourage him. I sometimes offered advice. I made him laugh at times. Rusty had insulated himself due to the divorce. He did not want anything else to hurt him. Slowly, I saw him emerge from that secret place and become more relaxed and confident. He was also becoming an excellent guitarist. I saw Rusty start healing and being his great, funny, sensitive self God always had intended him to be. The ultimate sign that he was confident came when he walked into a lesson with the tablature to "Free Bird" by Lynard Skynard. He wanted to learn the song. I nearly fainted. This is one of the most difficult rock guitar songs to play, especially the lead part. He was ready!

Measure by measure, breaking it down each week, we worked on it. We were still working on it when I left Tom's Creek. I can tell you that today Rusty can play that song note for note now. He learned it. His confidence soared and there is nothing he cannot tackle now on guitar.

Through him, Britt and I also began to bond. He walked into my office one Sunday after church and announced to me that he was going to be a drummer. I expressed to him that I thought that was a really cool thing. He also, in his own youthful cocky way, told me he could write a song about anything. So I decided to challenge him. "Okay!" I said. "Write a song entitled 'I'm Gonna Be the Drummer for Jesus in His Holy Ghost Rock and Roll Band.'" He smiled and took the challenge and walked out the door.

My life and their lives would be bound together again. God had laid the groundwork at Tom's Creek for further ministry to and with those boys. God always knows what He is doing. God always knows where He is going. God sets us up in ways we cannot even begin to see at the time He is setting us up. Invest in the lives of students. Actively seek ways to minister to them. Build relationships. You never know what God may be planning down the road, or how God will use you to point a kid to be their best for God. Love students if they are quiet and hurt. Love them if they are cocky and rude. Love them if they trash a classroom.

There were surely other students at Tom's Creek. We began an R.A. basketball league for both Middle and High School boys and the Baptist churches in the area played one another on Saturdays. I coached one of our Middle School boy teams. They were good. Kevin Dobbs was brought onto the team by Eddie! Kevin became a great ball player. The ministry was growing. New kids were showing up weekly on Wednesday nights. Josh Kosko was one of them. Here was a 14 year-old full of potential but shipwrecked due to his circumstances. He was living with his mom and his grandmother, his twin sister, and his younger brother just up the road from the church. Josh became my shadow.

Josh had no father in the home. Their dad walked out on them when they were babies. Mom had her own issues. Josh had a drug addiction problem. He had gotten involved with one of the "gangs" in Stephens County. He thought sex was something people just did. He was totally devoid of any moral boundaries. He had stolen. He had been a vandal. He had put anything into his body you could name, practically. Again, it was as if the enemy through Josh was saying to me, "Okay. Do you want to love students unconditionally? LOVE THIS!" I did love Josh. He saw

Jesus through Tom's Creek and in my life and the lives of some students there and was saved.

When he came at an invitation to tell the pastor he wanted Jesus, he was refreshingly not "churched." When the pastor questioned him before the church if Josh wanted to be saved, Josh replied something on the order of "shoot yeah!" The whole church laughed. How refreshing to see a totally new Christian who had not become jaded to church games and church language!

Josh is one of the smartest kids I have ever met. He is extremely intelligent. He has a bent for music and the arts. He draws beautifully. He can sing. He plays bass. He writes poetry. Josh would come to the church after school and just hang out with me. He would watch as I programmed my keyboard with tracks for praise choruses. He would sing with me. There was a bond between us that was deeper than I ever imagined at the time.

One afternoon while Josh and I were in the student area working with the keyboard, Sandy, one of the young men of the church came rushing in out of breath and very excited. There had been a wreck down the road from the church and Eddie was involved in it. I told Sandy to go to Eddie's home and tell his parents about it and for them to please meet me at the accident because that is where I would be, with Eddie.

Josh and I jumped into the car and headed toward Toccoa on Tom's Creek Road. As we approached the curve at the Fieldale chicken plant I could tell this was not going to be good, so I told Josh I was taking him home, as he lived nearby. I just had a feeling Josh did not need to see this. I returned quickly to the scene, found a police officer, and told him I was the student pastor of Eddie and that Eddie had been calling for me. He pointed me to an ambulance. Eddie had heard my voice and started crying out for me. I entered the back of the ambulance and there he was . . . along with Kevin also. They both were crying and begging me to pray for them. I immediately prayed for them, partially to calm them, but also to seriously call out to God on their behalf. The Emergency Medical Technician there with us told me they would be fine, but needed to go in for observation just to be sure. I left the ambulance, thanked the EMT for allowing me time with them, got in my car, and left because I was to meet the pastor and visiting evangelist for our revival at a restaurant in town. Little did I know that hidden from my view was another tragedy lying in the grass by the side of the road.

I met the pastor, Hazel, and the evangelist at the restaurant. We were bantering with small talk, even mentioning the wreck, when the church secretary walked into the restaurant with a look of horror on her face. She approached the table and knew this was going to be bad. She told us that we needed to get to the hospital. She had gotten a call that one of our teenagers from the church had been killed in an accident near the church. Because Clack had no cell phone, the church member who found out called her because she always knew our schedules. I looked at her and told her I had just left that wreck from praying with Eddie and Kevin. She sadly looked at me and told me that it was not either of them, but Joseph.

Joseph was one of my best kids at the church. He had lived his faith quietly. Everyone at the middle school knew him. They also knew he was a Christian. You never heard anything out of the way concerning Joe. I was praying to God that this was all a big mix-up in the chaos of the wreck. The evangelist offered to go ahead with the service and just "handle things" while Clack and I went to the hospital to be with the family.

We apologized to the waitress for leaving. The evangelist stayed and had a meal at our request. Clack and I made a beeline for the hospital.

Kids from school had already begun to gather. Police were holding them at bay outside. I talked to one of the officers and pushed my way past the students and into the hallway. As I entered the private waiting area there, my eyes fell on Gail, head in hands, sitting and giving glory to God, thanking him for the years they had been allowed to have Joseph. Her husband, Danny, was right by her side. I just hugged necks, expressed my love to them, and sat quietly with them. I could not believe the strength from that Godly mother. She repeatedly praised God for His goodness. They were waiting on a doctor for official word about their son.

When the doctor arrived he was very kind to the family. He carefully told them that there had to be an official identification. Who would go to the morgue and make a positive identification? Danny broke down. Through tears he said, "I will." "Danny," I asked, "do you want someone to go and stand with you?" Danny and I silently walked shoulder to shoulder down a hallway that seemed a mile long. The moment we entered the morgue I saw a very familiar pair of hiking boots exposed from under the cover of a body. I knew those boots. Those belonged to Joe.

The doctor came and as gently as he could he prepared us for what we were about to see. As the sheet was pulled back, there was Joseph, braces and all. He was swollen from the injuries to his face but it was definitely

Joseph. I broke down and began to quietly weep. Danny, in a moment of parental denial and disbelief, asked me if it were really Joe. I could barely squeak out an affirmative. When I did, he began to cry and sob again, calling out his son's name. I just stood there with my arms tightly around Danny's shoulder and we both wept in our shock and emptiness that someone we loved was gone.

Now, we had to break it to his mother one more time. Danny told her. Through a mother's tears she again began to give glory to God for being allowed the privilege to have Joseph as a gift from Him for 15 years. I was totally broken, lamenting the loss of Joseph, my friend and one of my best teen students. The following days would stretch me to the limits of physical, emotional, and spiritual endurance. Two others also lay dead from that wreck. A church member's elderly father had also died, totally unrelated to the wrecks. The day after the wreck was going to be a day of ministry forever burned into my mind.

I arrived home from the hospital, grieving, empty, emotionally exhausted, and feeling almost physically sick. In one incident, three of my students' lives were impacted forever, especially Joe's life. Joe had gotten into the Volkswagen with his friend, whose father was driving them home from school. Joseph had never ridden home with them before, but had always taken the bus home from school. Eddie was coming home from school with Kevin and another friend in a truck. Joseph's friend's father decided to stop at Fieldale where he worked to pick up a check. While turning into the road from the plant the truck rounded the curve and hit them, killing Joseph, the father, the son, and injuring the boys in the truck.

I had just settled into the bed that evening when the phone rang. It was the principal of Stephens County Middle School. He was putting together a team of ministers/ counselors for school tomorrow to help the students deal with their grief. He asked me to join them. I told him I would be there for the meeting before the students started arriving. I hung up the phone and pretended to sleep.

The following day at the middle school students arrived to news of Joe's death. Our job was to listen, console, watch the students and just basically get them through the day. There were groups that would gather in the halls. Some would then reform in the cafeteria or a classroom. I remember sitting with one class of 8th graders and just asked them to tell me all they knew and remembered about Joe. The girls naturally opened up first about how much they liked him, how funny he was, and how good he was. It was a challenge to keep the students inside, out of the halls, and in classrooms so they could be better cared for and contained. Toward the end of the day I walked up on something in the 8th grade hall that took my breath away. Students have such unique ways of expressing their grief and loss and love!

I noticed some boys down on their knees and doing something inside a bottom locker. When I asked I discovered that they had taken the door off Joe's locker. They did not know his combination so they just removed the whole door. They gathered all of Joes' books and belongings and had taken them to the office for Joe's parents to receive. They had then returned to the locker and began signing it inside and outside with notes to Joe. I joined them in signing the locker. I stood there and watched as student after student came and knelt and found a place to at least sign their names. This was a moving tribute to a young life well-lived. We all were crying.

I shall never forget that day. We, the counselors and the students, got each other through it. We cried together, talked about Joseph's life together, and even laughed at times. The funerals were yet to come. I would attend four funerals in three days.

I do not remember much about Joe's funeral. I just remember his parents asked me to sing, which I did. I remember the huge crowd. I remember the long drive to his burial spot. I also remember attending that father's funeral, his son's funeral, and the funeral of the elderly man who had also died.

God got me through it. The toughest thing I have ever had to do in ministry was to stand with Danny Jameson as he identified his son's lifeless body. I pray I never have to do that again. The emotions I felt and that I saw in him are indescribable. There is no way to adequately put it into words. I had weathered that storm well. I felt I did all I could as a minister to help a community through a tragedy. The church had come through that storm well. Another storm was coming, one that would test my character and belief like never before.

As the student ministry grew, it began to attract a larger circle of students, including black teenagers. They began coming and worshiping with our student group. I could do nothing but welcome them. I had not pursued them at all. God was drawing them to that place.

During the interview process preparing to come to Tom's Creek, I was asked a question that should have been a red flag to me even then. They wanted to know that I would not actively pursue black people to come to church there. My answer was simple. If they came it would be God sending them because I would have my hands full with the white students. When the black students began to come, the grumbling began.

I was called to a deacon's meeting. They asked me to "tell those boys to find a place to worship with their own kind." I told them I could not do that. That set them back on their heels. I further explained that they just started showing up. God was bringing them in. I then boldly told them that if they wanted God to take His hands off the church just begin telling the Holy Spirit who he can and cannot send to the church. The pastor backed me up. He told the deacons in no uncertain terms that I was right and they were wrong. That ended the meeting.

After that, some of the teen boys for reasons not fully known were accused of being in town, threatening the black kids and trying to stir up trouble. After facing that down and calming the waters, the deacons sent a tearful chairman to me to tell me that things just were not working out. My pastor and I were saddened. The deacon chairman was obviously broken and did not want to be the bearer of bad news. I tied up loose ends over the next few weeks that followed and prepared to move to the next church, Poplar Springs Baptist Church. Toms' Creek is a great church. I was saddened that they were short-sighted in their vision of reaching the community for Christ. Perhaps the seeds were sown for them to love everyone unconditionally.

CHAPTER TWELVE

HALL COUNTY: THE POPLAR SPRINGS YEARS

Poplar Springs seemed eager to talk with me and to get me on board. The worship ministry was in shambles. The student ministry basically consisted of the missions organizations. In the beginning, it seemed like a good fit. I knew I had the skills and call of God on my life to raise the bar and make those ministries there highly effective. The pastor, David, was from my "neck of the woods" in South Georgia. He grew up in Chula and often came to Sycamore as a child with his dad to the peanut mill. There was no reason this church could not flourish under our leadership.

And so I began to develop a thriving ministry to students. I began visiting South Hall Middle School regularly where David's son attended to build relationships with students there who would hopefully check out the student ministry of the church. Kids began coming. I developed as relevant and attractive a meeting for students on Wednesday nights as I could. Kids who had dropped out of that church began coming back. New students from South Hall and Johnson schools began to attend.

The worship ministry began to take off. The choir there was full of talent. They sounded great and responded to my leadership. Numbers grew. I began to move the music from totally "southern gospel" to more contemporary styles. I used old hymns and gospel songs couched in more modern arrangements. In my heart I knew I was on the right track. What I did not know initially was that I had landed in the middle of a church full of some of the meanest people in Hall County. This was a church happy as a clam just the way they were, and they were not about to change.

In this congregation were some of the worst gossipers and backstabbers I have met in all my years of ministry.

The students were growing in their faith. They were bringing others. The student meeting was powerful. We would sing and worship, pray, and then I would offer them a strong challenge from God's Word. There were special events for them. I brought in bands I knew for special lock-ins. The ministry there was taking off like a rocket . . . and threatening the adults like you would not believe.

Three brothers, John, Bobby, and Richard, came to be a part of us. These boys were a mess, not really churched even though they had been to another church before. When these boys and a few others showed up, that church's preconceived idea that ministry is always a neat little package that rocks no one's boat went right out the window. Any man of God knows that ministry can be very messy. The student ministry at Poplar Springs got very messy. It upset the status quo. It also revealed how immature the adults at Poplar Springs were. When you are dealing with people, they drag all their baggage right into the church with them. This is a strong statement, but one I stand by. Satan had his minions, his people in that church just waiting to start howling and criticizing and finding ways to neutralize my ministry should it happen to really have God's hand on it. I was in for a clash that went on under the surface. It was ugly. It was dishonest. It was right out of the pit of hell.

Let the messiness begin. In my student group were two 7th grade girls. Both were very sharp kids. They were intelligent, beautiful, and on the surface very loving. Both came from good homes with good parents. These two girls began a feud at school that began to carry over into the church and the student group. They did nothing but fight constantly. It became so intense that the parents asked me to intervene. After talking with the parents and understanding what I could, I talked with both girls. Just when I thought the problem was solved, they began the feud all over again. David and I both then intervened again. The students were taking sides. The student group was splitting over it. Unfortunately, this was one feud that I had to minister "around" because I could not solve it. They insisted on hating one another. The feud lasted through their Senior year at Johnson High School.

Two other girls lived to gossip and spread rumor, innuendo, and outright lies about people in the church. They did not confine their poisonous activity to other students, but also went after adults at times they did not like. These girls smiled at you while they were stabbing you in the back. I was never able to get a handle on these two either, as they insisted on ruining reputations.

The messiness continued the summer I took the students to Panama City Beach for a week-long retreat. John, Richard, and Bobby signed up to go. I needed a band to play down there for the kids in their worship. I decided to form a praise band just for the retreat. I called Rusty Richards from Tom's Creek who was now 17 and asked him if he would be my lead guitarist. His brother Britt had gotten skilled at drumming and we put him in the band as our drummer. Josh, my "adopted" son, was skilled at bass. I would ride the keyboards and handle the vocals. And so, HIGHER POWER was born. I realized I was at a point in my ministry where former students such as these were now young adults and I was calling out their gifts and ministering to them in a whole new way. I was also giving them a piece of the ministry God called me to and ministering alongside them.

The student group pulled out for Panama City early in the morning. I was driving the van with the younger students in it. Richard was sitting behind me in the van. We were barely getting started on the journey when I realized that the window behind me was open, and it was starting to rain, and the wind from the window was very loud and bothering my head. I asked Richard to close the window. Somehow, he pulled one side of the window one way and the girl with him pulled the other side the other way, and the window shattered. The girl had a very minor scratch from the accident. Glass shards were all over the place. Rain was coming into the van. I had no place to stop. Checking on the girl occasionally I pulled into a place as quickly as I could find one. We took care of her minor scratch. We got as much of the glass out of the van as we could. We took a trash bag and duct tape and covered the window to keep the rain out. Now I had another issue. Going down the road the trash bag made this deafening flapping noise. I was not happy and blessed inside. If this was happening and we had not even gotten out of Georgia, what on earth would happen during the week?

I have also learned to get students to the bathrooms and try to go whether they have to or not before leaving on a trip. One girl had to go to the bathroom every 20 minutes during the trip down. When you have 40 teens and adults traveling together and stop, that stop is going to cost you 15 or 20 minutes of travel time. An 8 hour trip turned into a 10 hour trip. It was a nightmare. I banned buying drinks eventually until we had arrived at the retreat site.

The rest of the week turned out well. HIGHER POWER was a hit with the kids. On Wednesday night God really broke through. Richard and Bobby were estranged brothers. Bobby was a great kid. He was the "Duh! Football!" type. He reminds me to this day of the cartoon character, the dog who used to always say, "Which way did he go, George? Which way did he go?" God began to prick Richard's heart about that relationship. In front of the whole group one evening Richard apologized to his brother for the way he had treated him, which broke Bobby's heart. In the end, all three brothers were hugging and crying and the student group wept with them.

Jamie, my Goth kid, sat at a picnic table that night after the service with me outside the assembly room. She had questions about God. Jamie was one of the brightest young ladies I have ever met. There was incredible pain in her life. Somewhere along the journey of her life, she had been seriously wounded through parental rejection. As we talked I could tell she desperately wanted the peace Jesus was offering her. Eventually that evening she prayed and became a follower of Jesus. She wanted to be baptized there at the retreat. After a phone call home for approval, the next evening Pastor David, who went on the trip with us, baptized her in our pool there. Others came to Christ that week also.

We returned home with new glass in the van. New believers were in those vans. Revived and reconciled Christians were riding home. But I was headed into a storm. I had already sensed that the enemy was motivating his forces. The people of the church could not have cared any less about how God moved in the kids' lives. All I heard was griping and complaining about the broken glass and the girl's cut.

Rick and Mary were members of that church. Mary joined choir. Mary second-guessed me and sought to provoke me every rehearsal. I just loved her and went on. One night at church, Rick and Mary came to me and offered to donate their piano to the church. We needed one in the new building, so I graciously accepted their offer. But, when the men went by their home to pick it up, they were not home. Somehow, communication had broken down. They got an attitude over it. Rick and Mary were in the Bell Choir rehearsal room and I stopped in on my way to choir to apologize to them for missing them in picking up the piano. Before I could complete my first sentence Rick started waving me off with his fat hand saying, "You just go on and do your thing." I was crushed. I had never felt such hatred from someone. I barely got through choir rehearsal. Rudene picked up on my sad spirit and after choir asked me what was wrong. I did not really want to say, but I told her what happened and how sad and hurt I was. Her reply was, "Don't worry about those two. That's just how they are. I'm kin to them and I know." I went home and cried that evening.

From there it was all downhill. People began to complain about the Wednesday evening worship music with the kids. It could not be Christian. It was too loud. It was rock. God only likes southern gospel. Someone actually had the nerve to say that to me. I just bit my tongue. That same criticism began to filter into the Sunday worship. They did not like the music. The Personnel Committee began their underhanded meetings after that. No matter what I did, they still called me in and complained. I toned things down. Even David fell for what was going on. The chair of the personnel committee, had I known then what I now know would have been toast when I was done with her. While she was self-righteously criticizing me in front of the committee and asking subtly threatening questions such as "do you like working here?" she was having an affair and eventually left her husband to pursue it. I would try to focus the committee and the church on the good things God was doing. Kids were being saved and baptized. Christian teens were growing in their faith. Worship music was better than it had ever been. Each time all they would dwell on was the broken van window, the loud music, the few boys who were rowdy on Wednesday nights after church, and gripe and complain about things that even 10 years later do not matter.

In the midst of that battle, God was using me in a way I never thought possible. Almost two years into my ministry at Poplar Springs, my phone rang at home one day. It was Josh Kosko from Toccoa, a former student of mine there. I had loved Josh and his twin sister, as well as his brother Danny deeply. I had not heard from Josh in two years. When he called my name on the phone he immediately began to weep. He told a story of how he had gotten back into drugs and a dangerous lifestyle since I had left Tom's Creek. The shocker caught me totally off-guard. He told me he needed to leave his home and Toccoa and make a fresh start. I nearly fainted when he asked, "Can I come live with you?"

I told him several things. First of all, I told him I was a bachelor and used to living alone and coming and going as I pleased. This would change things for me, added responsibility. I was not sure what my legal grounds were. I told him that he would be required to achieve certain goals and behaviors that it would not be easy. He begged further. I asked him to give me a week to think and pray and talk to some people I trust concerning this. I would call him in a week.

I talked to Pastor David. I talked to a lawyer. I talked with my parents. Then, I sat down and drew up a contract between me and Josh and his mom. On a Sunday after church I met Josh and his mother at Curt's in Oakwood to talk with them and be clear what the expectations were. They read the contract. In that contract were the things I expected of Josh and the consequences of violating the contract. I expected Josh to either enroll at Johnson High School or get his GED. I expected Josh to get a job and help with the finances at home. There was to be no drugs and alcohol in my home, nor were there to be females present when I was gone, and even then, they were to NEVER be upstairs alone in his bedroom. He was expected to attend church every Sunday. He and his mom signed the contract and I became Josh's legal guardian.

A week later Josh moved in. A separate book should be written about Josh. Josh worked hard and got his GED. He helped financially in the home, working in restaurants after a short stint with Food Lion. He began to grow in his faith. He surrounded himself with Christian friends. He broke off all ties with Toccoa, except occasional phone calls to his mother and family. He was developing nicely as a bass player. He was deeply committed to that. He would come home at night and often practice and play bass until bedtime. He would play mornings until time for work. When it came time to form that band for the Panama City Retreat, Josh became the bass player. He became a MAJOR contributor to the music of HIGHER POWER later.

I received a phone call one day from Steven Lackey. Steven was the kid in the truck from Second Avenue Baptist Church in Rome who only rarely came inside to the student meetings. Steven had good news. He was getting married. He wanted me to know and asked me if I would do the honor of performing the ceremony. I shared with him that I do not do weddings without at least three sessions of council. He and his fiancée were two hours away. I asked him how we could possibly work that out. He was willing to drive the distance to Gainesville in order for me to do the ceremony. I hung up the phone. I was honored. I was also surprised. I began to prepare for their counseling. I gave Dr. Ken Ross, the pastor of Second Avenue Baptist Church at the time a courtesy call to be sure it was okay for me to do the service there at the church as Steven wanted.

They arrived for their first session. Steven showed up clean and sober, with a faith that was obviously growing. I was delighted to see him as a young man now in control of his life. His bride-to-be was attractive and sweet. We dealt with a painful past. She showed me a lot of courage. I sat there during the first session curious and bursting to ask Steven a question. As I was beginning to wrap up that session I sat back and looked at Steven and asked him, "Why did you choose me to do your wedding when you have Dr. Ross more than capable of doing the ceremony right there at Second Avenue?" Steven paused for moment, leaned forward in his chair, dropped his head, then looked up at me and here is what he said.

"Do you remember all those times I showed up and just sat in my truck at church? All the students would be there on the lawn talking and you would always come to my truck and talk to me. I want you to do my wedding because, I don't know, you always had a way of jumping over that fence and coming to where I was." There was the lump in the throat as I choked back tears. All I could say was "Thank you." The wedding was a great day. His parents were so good to me. I will always remember Steven and the lesson he taught me about unconditional love.

Look for those fences. Whatever you have to do as long as it is not immoral or illegal, find a way to get over that fence to the teens on the other side. Many of them only get conditional love at home. Parental love seems based on the performance of the child. Students need to see adults who love them just as they are but are not content to leave them like they found them. The Steven's and the Josh's of the world need adults who are willing to sacrifice time and energy, and even their lives if necessary to show students there is another way to live. There is real love. His name is Jesus. He lives in us.

The storm continued to build and roll. The Personnel Committee continued its mission of seeing to it that I was no longer welcome. Josh was never brought up in those meetings with me. I knew he was part of their dilemma. Josh was different. Josh liked his music hardcore. Josh had his ears pierced and had a few tattoos. He dressed in the baggy Jenko jeans. He was a loud kid who lived life loudly, talked loudly, laughed loudly, and scared the adults in that church nearly to death because of his "style."

The committee, the pastor, and I could never figure out what the problem was. I was faithfully ministering as God led me; I was not involved in anything underhanded and immoral. Then, after the last meeting I was talking to David about all the negativity and it hit us both almost at the same time. Poplar Springs and I were a bad fit. It was nothing more than that. My personality and the make-up and temperament of the church never had meshed. I had visited the schools weekly, loved the students, been faithful, worked the worship ministry to a whole new level, and the church just did not like ME. WOW! I offered David my resignation and prepared to leave. The worst was even yet to come.

The next day I sat down with Josh and told him that I was leaving Poplar Springs and that his role was to let no one know until after my resignation was made public. The agreement was the usual one. I resigned to the pastor since he was my direct supervisor. The resignation would remain confidential until I had another place to serve, then the resignation would be announced to the church. I told Josh that it may mean I move out of the county, even out of the state if God called me elsewhere. I also counseled him that he should consider what he will do in event of a huge move on my part. Josh was welcome to go with me wherever I went, but I wanted him to consider all his options. I then went into a period of prayer, asking God to show me the right door. God was about to put a man in my life that I had known on a fair friend level, but did not really know.

Charles Billingsley was booked to do a concert at Grace Baptist Church in Gainesville. The pastor, Rev. Chuck Nation, called me and asked me if I would come and run the sound for Charles. He knew my reputation around town with HIGHER POWER and as a musician and for some reason he felt I was the one. I arrived at the church the evening of the concert and sat with Charles at the little console in the corner of that small auditorium talking over the concert as we patched his mini-disc player into the system. We did sound check and all was well. I had him sounding as good as I could, especially with the limitations of that sound system. There was not enough wattage overhead, no graphic equalizer, no FX unit, and I was back in a corner.

The doors opened for the concert. Teenagers came into the auditorium of that church in drove after drove. It totally packed out and people were outside the door and others turned away due to the immense crowd. The audience was excited. I was about to be excited and not in a good way. Pastor Chuck walked onstage and introduced Charles. When Charles hit the stage the audience stood up applauding and yelling and clapping as the track to Charles' first song pumped through the speakers. I immediately had two problems. I could not see Charles for visual cues of things he might need in the monitors. I also could not hear him because the audience was louder than the sound system could ever be. I rode the board that concert by the seat of my pants, making educated guesses as to what was going on up there with Charles. We pulled it off! Afterward, Charles was hanging out with some of the kids and with me down in the fellowship area of the church. As the students cleared he went to his product table, picked up a CD, handed it to me and thanked me for doing such a hard job well. He handed me the CD and said, "Here! You have earned this tonight!" We both had a good laugh.

Now I was looking for another place to serve, but had not really gotten my resume out there when my office phone rang. On the other end was Chuck Nation, who had since taken the pastorate of First Baptist Flowery Branch just six miles up the road. He had been in a pastor's meeting and, as he put it, "had gotten wind" that I may be looking for a place to serve. He wanted to talk with me about joining him at Flowery Branch. We set up a meeting.

I met Chuck for lunch at Red Lobster in Gainesville. He was offering me the position of student and worship leader at Flowery Branch. He shared with me how that church had been through a tough split and was beginning to heal. The student ministry was in shambles. His dear wife had been able to develop and keep a core group of great students. He wanted me to rebuild that ministry. Worship was "a joke." He asked me to come and restore worship to its proper place. I told him I was honored, but why did he choose me? He looked at me in his low-key way and said, "I have been watching you ever since you came to Gainesville and I know you can do this."

God has a sense of humor. I had been praying that God would allow me to minister in a place closer to my parents if it was in His plan and purpose for my life to do so now. Here was Chuck offering me a position six miles closer to home. God is good. I met with their search committee. I met with their students and fell in love with them immediately. I led a service there and it felt good and right. And it was. Flowery Branch extended a call to me which I enthusiastically accepted. I did not even have to move! Josh could continue living with me. God had heard our prayers.

Meanwhile back at Poplar Springs I was preparing to say goodbye to the kids and break the news to them in the student meeting one hour before the service where I would resign to join Flowery Branch. It seemed like a good idea at the time for me to write every one of them a personal note of love and encouragement for their lives. I applauded their strengths and encouraged them to work on areas of weakness I knew were there. It was a tearful meeting. Students were hugging my neck and all was right until kids showed their parents the notes. Some of the parents became irate that I would stoop so low as to point out their children's weaknesses. They took the encouragement to keep growing and working on weak areas as a slam on their kids. I could not believe it. What I had meant for nothing but good turned into a parade of parents railing on me. The service came and I resigned, walked out the side door, and got into my car to leave. One of the fathers stood in front of my car because he had something he wanted to say. Now, his daughter was one of the worst in the group as far as attitude is concerned. She needed much encouragement to develop positive attitudes and to deal with an issue she had with one other girl in the group.

Her dad totally took me by surprise. His attitude was basically "after all we have been through I can't believe you would do this to my daughter. She is devastated and I am so angry with you." I looked at him and told him I was sorry but that I stood by what was in the letter. I rolled up my window and drove away, lest things escalate further. A few parents were very pleased with what I had said to their teen, but several were very upset. I have never seen a church that could take something so positive and totally twist it into something negative and damning. They did it toward worship. They did it after the Panama City trip. They had even managed to take a goodbye to the students I intended to be positive, loving, and meaningful, and make it into something ugly. I will never figure out people, especially that bunch at Poplar Springs.

Poplar Springs turned out to be the meanest group of Christians I have ever had to deal with. They could smile at you and be totally undoing your ministry behind your back. They could take positive things and focus in on one minor, insignificant thing that is inconsequential and blow it into a major issue, totally ruining the positive aspect of the event. They would say nasty things to your face that were not in a Christian spirit. They were definitely satisfied with the way things were at Poplar Springs and they were not about to change. They would attack, lie, get attitude, doing whatever it took to keep "their church" exactly like it was. When the new building was built, there was a man the students nicknamed the "Kitchen Nazi." The new kitchen was part of the new and very nice fellowship hall Poplar

Springs built while I was on staff there. He was adamant about keeping the kitchen and hall exactly like it was. He would pitch a fit when the students wanted to do something there. To him, nice unspoiled paint on the wall was more important than one soul who might come there for a teen event and be saved. As for me, I think you can always repaint a wall. You may only have one chance at keeping a soul from hell. We did a Christmas musical there, which meant building a stage and installing lights. Again, it was a battle with the Kitchen Nazi to get that done. This was a church of the status quo. They did not want to change. Had I been Pastor David I would have left that church a long time ago. He is more patient than I will ever be. As I write this five years after leaving that place, David remains a very loving and good pastor to a people who desperately need it. My life was now turned to the task at hand in Flowery Branch. God would give me a ministry there like no other. Much would be accomplished. The next five years would see many victories won in a church too eager to grow physically before they grew numerically. These would be remarkable years.

CHAPTER THIRTEEN

HALL COUNTY: THE FLOWERY BRANCH YEARS

About a dozen students met with me that first Wednesday night. Their small room with four classrooms off that room was all painted with murals and "teen" stuff.

It was interesting but ugly. The students had painted it. It was important to this group. Those walls would remain painted like that for some time.

In that group of students were teens like Keith Crandall, Stacia Ertzberger, James Nation, Chris Moore, Jeanette Crandall, Chase Ertzberger, and others. Chuck's wife Susan had done a good job of developing a core group of students from which to build. This group had been discouraged and mistreated in ways that had demoralized them. Some had scattered, never to return. With guitar in hand and keyboard programmed in front of me I introduced them to a form of worship they had not experienced in their group before. I began to build relationships with them. They learned to trust me. The foundation for an explosion of people was being laid.

Worship in that church was non-existent. People gathered Sunday after Sunday and sang songs, went through the motions, then went back home unchanged. I can say with certainty that God's heart was broken over this. My first rehearsal with the choir brought me face-to-face with about 10 people who had been told they had no talent, they would never be a good choir, and week after week had been verbally abused to the point they had no self-confidence. When they first opened their mouths to sing, I was shocked. The potential was incredible. How could anyone say there was no talent there? Deb Crandall's rich alto voice was smooth and beautiful and flowed easily from her. Her faith showed on her face as she sang. I discovered she had traveled with The Continental Singers! Skip West on the back row there had a powerful tenor voice. With just a few adjustments Skip would be a wonderful singer. The pastor's wife, Susan, sang with beauty. Her almost flawless soft soprano voice had the sounds of quiet praise music all over it. Another lady, Ann Marie Barnes had a great voice that lent itself more to traditional gospel songs, a lovely voice. And there was Mary Radford. Mary was not a soloist, but Mary had a good voice. Mary brought a great faith in God and faithfulness to her church and worship that we really needed to see. God was going to use a poor, lost soul, saved by the grace of God and gifted with music to totally transform this choir. God was up to something good.

I began to visit West Hall High School every Friday during lunch to see my students and hook into others who needed Jesus. I was free to float from table to table and to talk with any student who wanted to talk. The only stipulation was that I could not evangelize. Any questions about God and religion had to be initiated by the student. Then, I was free to answer their questions.

The principal at that school had become known as "the stealth principal." Dr. Pirkle was rarely seen at the school. The joke among the students was that he was afraid of them and spent the day in his office hiding under his desk. He retired when I was three years into visiting that school. During that time I saw him twice. My first meeting with him was in the cafeteria. He shook my hand and called me by name. He was more in touch with what was going on than students imagined. He wanted me to know he appreciated me being there and asked me to please continue to visit and do what I was doing.

The second time I talked with Dr. Pirkle he became much more specific concerning the needs of his students. As we sat at a cafeteria table that day he began to point out students around us. "He could really use some time with you," he would say about one. He would show me another student and tell me, "This guy really needs some help." He was telling me without actually saying so, that he was concerned for their souls, too. I left that day with a new respect for Dr. Pirkle.

Through James Nation I met the jocks. James was on the football team. I would sit at their table and listen to their cocky, testosterone-infested banter. Soon some of them were showing up on Wednesdays and at special events. One thing that had started before I got there was a Sunday afternoon football game. The guys from the church would gather on the church property with some of the men and play football on the field we owned that was huge, just like a football field. That ran its course and eventually stopped, but it served a great purpose for a long time to get guys introduced to the church.

Keith Crandall was a member of the band. His sister was in the flag corp. Through those students I began to meet the band members and hook into them. Stacia was really popular and introduced me to both guy friends and some of her female buddies as well.

So, my "fame" began to spread through the school. They began to expect me to be there every Friday. They would ask me to stay for a pep rally or for the homecoming parade and rally each year, which was hysterical. I have never had so much fun! And so, I became known as the unofficial chaplain of West Hall. There is a trickle-down effect that student pastors must be aware of if you get into a high school to visit. Your middle school students are going to eventually ask you why you have not visited them at their school and demand that you show up. If you do not begin a ministry to middle schools you will have missed an opportunity to reach more kids for Christ than you could ever have imagined.

But, it all began with me at West Hall High School in Oakwood, Georgia. God has used me more than I could have ever imagined. Seven years down the road I am still in touch with students from West Hall High School. Each Friday as I walked into that school I realized that God put those students in my path for a reason. I would breathe a prayer as I walked across the bus lanes to the school each Friday. What follows are stories and events, ministry and loving students no matter what.

When you walk into a building holding 1,300 students you will meet all kinds. During the lunch periods I would see tables of jocks, the girls' softball team, cheerleaders, the skaters, nobody's, the rednecks, the gay and lesbian tables, and the Goths and freaks. You see white students, black students, mixed race students, Hispanic and Mexican kids, Asian people; all the colors of melanin are there. Every world view and lifestyle is present. I believe without question that a student pastor must immerse themselves in the culture of students if we are to effectively minister to them. What better place than their school gives us the opportunity to do that?

I was visiting one day with some of the wrestlers at their table. As I got up I heard my name being called from across the cafeteria. When I got my bearings I realized that my summons had come from a table of Goth students. As I walked toward the table they said, "Hey, come talk to us." I pulled up a chair and met Wesley and William, along with all the others at that table dressed in black, girls and guys. These became my good friends. I liked this group of students because at least they were real. They did not play games with me. "Why do you come here?" was quickly asked of me. I told them unapologetically that I was the student pastor of 1st Baptist Flowery Branch and I just loved visiting with students. "Well, you never talk to us," they responded. I looked Wes in the eye and told him, "I'm here now, so let's talk." As I got to know them more and more each week I saw a group of students there who were wounded. All were from similar broken family backgrounds. I never knew from one week to the next what color hair William would have, how it would be "styled," or if he would even have hair! They needed the love of Jesus. In my own way I shared that with them. I laughed with them. They talked about some funny stuff! They did some really off-the- wall things with food.

The Goths were some of my favorite people there. They were politically savvy to a point. Though we were at opposite ends of the spectrum in our political beliefs, because I gave them the courtesy of an honest listen, they would hear my views. We had some good political discussions together some Fridays. There were spiritual questions they would ask. I would answer their questions honestly. I knew they were seeking something that is real. It was clear that the black clothing, the pale make-up with black eye color, and the piercings were merely outward cries of a soul inside that was hurt, wounded, and dark and crying out for hope. So, I just loved them and planted seed into their lives. Some of them began to come to some of the special events we did for students like mega-lock-ins and concerts. God was working.

Every week they would call my name and wave me over to their table. One Friday I just point-blank asked them a question that I had thought about for a long time. I asked them why they always wanted me to sit at their table when I was pushing 50 and they were teenagers, when I was a Christian and they were not even sure they believed in God. We had nothing in common. Why? Their response humbled me and made me angry at the same time. I wanted to cry. They told me that I was the only student pastor that would talk to them. When others would visit, they would look at them like they had some "disease" and just walk on by. They told me that I actually would sit and talk to them. They told me they liked me. They said that I was different.

A sidebar is in order here. Student pastor, do not neglect "the least of these." Emo and Goth students need the love of God shown to them. They often come from abusive backgrounds. They will come from single-parent homes. Their father will often be absent either physically from the home or emotionally absent. They have been hurt deeply. They see the effect of sin on the world, but to them it's just that life is unfair, it is painful, and they can't wait to die. One emo kid's slogan for a time was, "We All Die! Why Wait?" They grieve deeply over their world of brokenness. The pain is deep and the pain is real. They look for someone who is real. They seek out people who understand their pain and will lovingly walk with them through the pain until it is behind them.

My fear is that we will lose a generation of the most sensitive, loving, and intelligent students the world has ever seen but for God doing a work among those who embrace the Goth and Emo lifestyles. These students cut themselves so that they can forget the pain of their souls by focusing on the pain of physically cutting themselves. They are merely trading one pain for another. They need to hear that Jesus was cut with the whip that laid his back open to feel their physical pain. They need to know that Jesus felt the same pain in his soul they feel when his Father turned His back on him when he was dying on the cross. Jesus has felt every emotion and pain that this generation feels. When I see Goth and Emo kids embrace this message of hope, they become just as passionate about Jesus as they did about being "Goth." They worship with passion. Their lives are wrapped around Jesus and others like them who know Jesus. They do not judge their friends still caught in the web of the Gothic lifestyle but they love them and seek to reach them in their own special way for Jesus. Please, student pastors, do not neglect "the least of these."

The worship ministry at Flowery Branch was beginning to find its wings. I wanted to develop an ensemble that would include brass and a rhythm section. As usual, students led the way. Two young boys, brothers, Drew and Chris Perkins stepped up. Drew was older, 13 and played trumpet at West Hall Middle School. Chris played trombone. I worked with them and they began accompanying the hymns in the service. The ensemble was always a work in progress. Musicians came and went. Then a family joined the church there I had known at Poplar Springs. Mike Leary brought his wife Madonna, his son Elgin, his daughter Megan, her sons Daniel and Doug, and their son Julian. It took me sometime when I first met them to sort out who belonged to who in this blended family. Elgin was a trumpet player who jumped at the opportunity to play in church. There was Christy, a trombone player from West Hall whose family had joined First Baptist. Daniel Phillips came to us to play French horn for awhile. Eventually he got a job requiring him to work Sundays and had to bow out. He did a great job while with us. Randy Searcy had become a fantastic bass guitarist and played bass. Derek Dunagan took the reigns at acoustic guitar after Rusty Richards of HIGHER POWER spent some months with us in the ensemble playing electric guitar. Phyllis Reeves was our pianist for the traditional hymns. Lana Perkins, and later, another lady was our organist. During the contemporary songs I was introducing to the church, I played the keyboards and did the vocals. God sent us a guy named Scott who faithfully played trumpet for a long time. He married eventually and he and his wife began attending a new church, a fresh start for them.

There was also a drummer. A young man named Jonathan Sanders began bringing his own set of drums each Sunday to play during the service. He was solid, faithful, and talented. Jonathan moved on, but there is a special place in this student pastor's heart for him because he was so very faithful. The pastor's youngest son John was taking lessons and began playing drums. In the beginning he was an immature learning drummer. He was young, only 14 at the time. He became one of the best drummers by 16 I have ever seen. Initially he had trouble establishing a tempo and holding it throughout the song. He also tried to play along with hymns and praise songs like a hard core drummer would. But he learned quickly. The ensemble eventually began playing throughout the service, traditional hymns and praise and worship songs on the contemporary edge. And that was the beginning of trouble.

There was a group of senior adults who sat in the back left corner of the church. Undoubtedly their Sunday Bible study consisted of a weekly discussion of those drums and the music in the worship. I never cease to wonder at the immaturity of supposedly grown, wise, older people. Oh! The games some play! First, the drums were too loud. A repositioning of them and putting them behind a plexi-glass shield took that argument away from them. Then they were silently refusing to stand and sing during the praise and worship time, complaining that they could not stand that long. I told them they were free to sit down if it became physically painful to stand that long. Everyone in the house would be on their feet . . . except that back corner, all seated with sour looks on their faces, the frozen chosen. They sent their mouthpiece, Jerome, to talk to me. I very diplomatically but clearly told him I was not going to change the music. Why? It was attracting the 40-under age group with kids to build the church on. Many, and I do mean many, had joined that fellowship because of the worship music there. So, I basically asked him if he was willing to lose half the church if I did change the music. He had no answer for that and left scratching his head. I have never been anyone's "yes" man and I was not about to begin now. The pastor stood his ground with them, also. We would stay the course. I would eventually be proven that I was 100% correct in what I said to Jerome that day.

Early on in my ministry there we installed a screen and projection system to run Power Point for hymn and praise chorus lyrics, as well as to show videos and run announcements prior to the service. One day prior to a Senior Adult luncheon some of the "blue hairs" cornered me. I use the term "blue hair" as a term of affection. They wanted to know if we really were going to put up that screen. The answer was yes. Their next question I had already prepared for, because I knew it would be coming. Why is it that older people hold the Baptist Hymnal at almost the same level of sanctity as God's Word? They wanted to know if I was going to remove the hymnals from the pews once the screen was up and running. I smiled at them. I told them that the hymnals would remain in the pews for those who wished to continue using them. I also went one step further and said the hymn numbers would no longer be announced, but would be listed in the printed worship order and on the opening frame of each hymn on the screen. The screen was an easy battle to fight and win. There was not much resistance. At first, a few complained that they could not read the words due to "busy" backgrounds. That issue was taken care of. Battle won.

Meanwhile, the church there had also decided to build a 1.3 million dollar building that would include new offices, classrooms, a huge commercial kitchen and fellowship hall that could be divided for smaller groups and opened to seat 500 if needed. The icing on the cake . . . the building would also include a gym. The building went up. The idea was that if we had more room and all this space and this gym and a nice fellowship hall people would come. Already, the students had moved out of their original meeting place in the old building to share a larger space occupied on Sundays by the Senior Adult Class. I already had my eye on the smaller part of the fellowship hall with the divider up once that building was finished as space for the students to do what I had always wanted to do there.

I have learned that the saying from the movie, "Field of Dreams" is not true. "If you build it, they will come" does not apply to churches. That is Hollywood drivel. First Baptist's idea was that people would come and join and give and help pay for the building if we built it. They had to learn the hard way. You do NOT build a building without counting the cost, and if it cannot be paid for, do not build it. Scripture teaches us this in a parable of the man who started a building without counting the cost. He did not have enough to finish it. The building sat half finished and wasted.

The way to build a building is to build people first. The church absolutely must come to the day when their focus is laser-sharp on people and not events and buildings. First Baptist can have two and three worship services on Sunday in their worship center, as well as multiple Sunday Schools, FIRST, before building an expensive building. Then when the base is there financially and you have counted the cost you build to better accommodate them. Another option is to begin cell groups for Bible study in homes and restaurants and coffee houses. It is PEOPLE who have to be built FIRST, not the building.

With the building finished I entered a new office with new furniture. It was nice and I was grateful for the office. It offered more privacy for study and planning. I had more desk top space. I am one who spreads out to work and when I have two or three big projects going at once I need a lot of space to put things. I had that.

The students continued to grow in number and in maturity as young Christians. We had our own area for Wednesday worship now in the new building. AWANA took off like a rocket in the new building, using the gym and rooms in the older building also. The students had been really patient with me, an older man with a guitar, leading them on Wednesdays in worship. My dream had always been to have a student praise band that took charge of the music in the student worship, freeing me up to do the talk only. I have always believed that the first thing students should see when they come into a room for student worship is students leading out in the worship, not the student pastor. Derek, Randy, and John stepped up again. They formed a student praise band. Derek really took charge. We had a sound system now. The church invested in a set of drums just for the student meeting area. Derek met with the band, taught them songs from Passion, Enter the Worship Circle, and other places. The band became really good! The students loved them and showed up weekly to hear them. I was free to plan my talk and instill God's Word into their lives. And so, every Wednesday night, the new building ROCKED with the sound of a great little praise band and students getting into it!

Somewhere in the midst of all the music and events and building I began to also visit West Hall Middle School. No ministry to students can flourish without reaching out to students in grades 6-8. They are awesome. I am not sure how it happened, but I found myself there helping out every Wednesday morning at 7:30 with 1st Priority, the Christian club that meets there. Scott Taylor, another student pastor, and I were the community volunteers for that club and the school. The kids found out that I was visiting the high school on Fridays during lunch and hit me up to visit them too. So, I dedicated Wednesdays to West Hall Middle School. After 1st Priority, I would eat breakfast somewhere, go to my office and plan worship and choir rehearsal, then at 11:00 I would return to the school, sign in, put my ID on, and go to the cafeteria and visit students through the whole lunch cycle. God opened so many doors of ministry there. He honored my efforts.

I am not really a mystic, but I had an experience one day while leaving the school that I cannot shake, nor merely write it off as my imagination. I do not even recall the exact date this happened, but probably during the 2002-2003 school year. I had visited the students from 11 till 1 p.m., signed out at the front office, turned my ID in and made the short walk to the front door. I began to stride toward the parking lot thinking about all those students with so many needs. I stopped and turned, looking at the school over my shoulder. "Ask me." I thought I heard a voice say that to me. "Ask me." A second time I heard it. I remember saying, "God, is that you?" "Go ahead. Ask me for it," He responded. "Ask you for what?" He then said something that floored me. "Ask me for this school and I will give it to you." I stood there and began crying, hoping no one was watching me. Then I prayed, "God, I want this school for you so badly. If you give me this school I will give it right back to you for your honor and glory, I promise. Thank you, God. Amen"

That became a turning point in my ministry. I drove home to lunch weeping uncontrollably. God had stepped into my life in the most unexpected way. West Hall Middle School was mine for God. What would I do with it? I faithfully stood at the door of the gym every Wednesday and called every kid by name and greeted them when they walked in for 1st Priority. I learned as many names as I could. They began to show up for ALIEN YOUTH, the Wednesday night meeting for students at First

Baptist. They came in droves to Mega-lock-ins I would do each year. Pretty soon everyone in the school, teachers and students alike knew my name. Doors of ministry swung wide open.

There was this really cute kid there named Josh. He had blonde hair and big blue eyes that made him look much more innocent than he was. When I first met him he was a smart-mouthed kid that always gave attitude. But I kept building a relationship with him, always speaking to him every week, joking with him, just spending time at his table. The day came when I sat at his table and he just looked at me with this scared, pale, look. As I reached over to shake his hand he blurted out, "I need to talk to you." I sat down and looked at him and said, "Okay." He then replied, "No, not here. Let's find someplace more private." I found a table in the cafeteria with no one sitting there and we parked across the table from each other.

His big blue eyes began to pool up with tears. He dropped his head. This 13 year- old was hurting. I was quiet until he could get himself together to speak. "Last night I had sex with my girlfriend for the first time ever, and I am so scared." And he was very afraid. He was afraid of their parents finding out. He was afraid she might be pregnant. Birth control was used but he was feeling guilty because he had not only taken something away from her but he had also given something he could never take back. He was broken. I let him talk and asked appropriate questions as I needed to. I then sought to lead him to understand something students just don't get in the heat of the moment.

Josh made a mistake, a sin. But it is not the end of the world. Josh had stepped outside of God's plan for him and sinned, thus the guilt and shame. Those two things are like God's alarm for us to let us know we are out of bounds. Even then, God loves us. He forgives us. He will help us deal with the fear. There is healing. I think Josh understood. I was in a school and could go no further with him. I gave him my phone numbers, e mail address, and AIM sign name if he needed to talk further. My relationship with Josh changed that day. Later, as a Freshman and Sophomore at West Hall High School, his attitude was one of deep respect and quiet love. I could see it in his eyes. Josh is going to make it.

J.D. was a cool kid. One day he just up and asked me to pray for his mother because she had cancer. I began praying that day, and every Wednesday at lunch I would ask J.D. how his mother was. There was Ryan. We all called him Boz, like "beaus." He was friends with Travis Clements, Brian Ernst, Caleb . . . you get the point. Those guys came to 1st Priority and became leaders. At lunch we all were "The Mob." I was inducted into the mob. What did I have to do? I had to drink a packet of hot sauce. Now, I love hot and spicy foods, so I knew this was not going to be difficult. The boys around that table had this look in their eyes that they had me. I think they were expecting me to gag and carry on and tear up and have to get water. I downed the packet and sat there and stared them down. With a collective "DANG" they expressed their disappointment.

But I was now one of "The Mob." We had a slogan of sorts: "God, Chicks, and Food, our three priorities."

1st Priority would see as many as 200 students show up. I cannot count the number of students I saw come to Christ in those meetings. Students would give their testimonies. Student pastors would come in and speak. Doug, the school custodian brought his guitar and harmonica and played several times, also sharing his testimony. I would bring my guitar and play and sing. Eventually Will English, Ryan "Boz" Bozarth, and I would play guitars together in those meetings along with a kid named Josh who is really good at keyboards. One morning I spoke to them on "Llamas To Put Into Your Life." This talk, by lunch, was all over the school.

Here is the Llama talk done "Reader's Digest" style. In Montana a sheep herder was having difficulty with coyotes invading and killing the sheep. This was a lady and she had tried everything. The coyotes would breach the fences. Watchdogs in the flock did no good either. One day, someone told her to invest in a llama and put it in the flock and that the llama would take care of business with the coyotes, guaranteed. She bought a llama and put it in the flock and the coyotes stopped invading and killing the sheep. Llamas are fearless and mean and would run the coyotes off. I then turned to talk about putting "llamas" in our lives to protect us, because Satan is like a coyote waiting to attack and devour us. I talked of God's Word, prayer, worship, and witness, as llamas to put into our lives. I also added that we need to be llamas to one another, protecting each other from the attacks of Satan. When I returned for lunch with the students, they greeted me with a new slogan that was all over the school . . . "Be the Llama!" They had gotten the message. In their humorous way they had invaded the whole school with my message to them.

Student pastors, be sure you are connecting with students in terms and language they understand. "Thees" and "Thous" do not connect. The term "getting saved" no longer connects with many students. They live in a world of technology that is potent. I wrestle with visuals, music, turns of phrase, computer technology, and even randomness, in order to be sure they "get it." For example, one evening in ALIEN YOUTH, my talk was entitled "What Are You Going To Do When the Deer Wakes Up?" This talk deals with friendships, forming friendships that will last and stand with us through the tough times. Just before I turned the talk to "who are you going to turn to when times get tough?" up on the screen in the student center came the clip from the movie "Tommyboy." It's the scene where they are riding along, enjoying life, singing, and having fun after putting a supposedly dead deer in the back seat of that convertible. In the middle of all their fun the deer wakes up and totally destroys the convertible. That scene ends with the two of them standing by the side of the road together, supporting one another. I then asked the question, "What are you going to do when the deer wakes up?" The message was plain that they needed Christian friends who would stand with them during that time. God has given us so many things at our disposal to use to communicate the gospel. I say let's use them all.

If you begin a ministry to a school, a good relationship with the principal is crucial to its success. Spend time with them. Minister to their needs as God opens doors. Both West Hall High and Middle Schools changed principals while I was ministering to those campuses. I managed to have good relationships with both new principals, as I had with both the exiting leadership. Dr. Sarah Justice, the woman who took the reigns at West Hall Middle School is an incredible lady. After a week of allowing the chaos of that first week of Middle School to settle into a routine, I made an appointment to visit with her. What transpired behind that closed door in the privacy of her office took me by total surprise. I already knew her in a way, as she was on staff there in a different position earlier. I simply offered my services to the school in any way possible. If there were a tragedy I would be available to come and help counsel.

She smiled and thanked me. She then told me she wanted me to keep doing what I had been doing in years past. I was free to visit the school during lunch and special events. She had been watching me and was impressed with how I related to the students. Then, she began to tear up. She asked me to pray for her. She shared with me how she became a Christian, how she was a woman of faith. She then said that she and her husband prayed daily for the students she was in charge of at West Hall Middle School. I then was on the verge of tears. I thank God for school leadership, who, at a time when it's not considered correct to express your faith openly in school, understand that prayer is the most powerful thing they can do to keep them centered and have wisdom to lead. I prayed with her that morning in her office. That Methodist lady is showing God's love to those students simply by the way she loves them on the campus there.

First Baptist had a growing worship ministry. One special evening the worship choir did a concert for the community with The Mike Speck Trio. Mike is a man very gifted by God musically. He can take the old songs and with the help of other arrangers wrap them in updated orchestration and they come alive all over again. The choir did six songs at the first of the evening. I had introduced Brooklyn Tabernacle Choir music to them, other black gospel music, as well as Mike Speck's arrangements. The worship center was packed out. The choir sang way beyond themselves. It was heavenly. The choir backed the trio on their songs when they came out to sing. Incredible! I still listen to the tape to this day and it helps me worship at times. A choir that had been told it had no talent was now backing one of the premier gospel groups in America and doing it quite well. To God be the glory!

Beneath the surface of a new building, a new associate pastor in Brian Skeggs, a growing and exciting worship ministry, and a student ministry that God was all over, there was trouble brewing.

The trouble brewing was this. The natives that sat in the left back corner of church were restless. They were giving Chuck fits about the music in worship. They were griping to him about "some of those kids" who were showing up on Wednesday nights and the loud music coming from the building. Chuck was not about to budge. The trouble also was that we had built it and they were not coming. No one was meeting the parents who would drop their kids off for AWANA and ALIEN YOUTH and inviting them to church and building relationships with them. The deacons were too busy fighting the pastor over a change in their roles as deacons to a more Scriptural one. The Senior Adults were not about to be out there with skateboards and bicycles and little kids, and loud music. Between AWANA and ALIEN YOUTH there would often be close to 150 kids in that building. Those kids had parents no one was reaching. No one wanted to reach them except Chuck, Brian, James, the AWANA Commander, and me. Those kids were messing up the building. There were hand prints and, GOD FORBID, foot prints on the fresh, new walls of the building. Here was a church where the building was more important than the people. You can always put a new coat of paint on a wall to cover the prints and bumps.

You cannot put a coat of paint on a soul that is battered and scarred with sin, especially if it slips into eternity and hell without the hope of Jesus. They missed it. Walls were more important than the souls of little children.

I had built over three years at West Hall Middle School a friendship with this kid named T.B. Now an 8th grader, T.B. was a skater kid who really seemed insecure about himself. His self-confidence seemed to really suffer. As the school year began to draw to a close in the spring of 2004, T.B. approached me in the cafeteria with a request that came from left field. He asked me if I would chaperon the 8th grade dance. Every spring, a dance was held just for the 8th graders to celebrate their move into High School. My first response was, "you can't be serious!" He was serious. In order to do this I needed to talk with the faculty sponsor of the dance. I asked him which teacher was the lead sponsor of the dance. "Mrs. Harris," he said. I started laughing. Mrs. Harris was one of the teacher sponsors of 1st Priority. I went to her and told her that T.B. had asked me if I would chaperon the dance. Would it be possible for me to chaperon and help in anyway she needed me? I was in!

That Saturday night was so much fun. All my young 8th grade buddies were there. Huston Gillis, Blake Anderson, and others showed up styling and profiling. Huston was dressed to kill. All the girls looked so pretty in their dresses, their hair done beautifully, and the make-up just perfect. I held purses for the girls, saved seats for guys, kept an eye on the dance floor and the hallways outside the cafeteria where the dance was held, took pictures for others and for myself . . . and became T.B.'s body guard.

T.B. sat quietly in a corner in the dark watching the crowd dance and pulse to the beat of the deejay's music. I would go over and talk with him. Later, some of his friends had joined him. Then, midway through the dance, here came some guys determined that T.B. was going to dance. They dragged him kicking and protesting to the dance floor, with me following them to be sure they were not going to hurt the kid and that T.B.'s objections were not so serious that he became angry or cried. Once he got out there he just stood there at first. The kids began to encourage him, gently taking his arms and moving thems to the music. Pretty soon, T.B. was enjoying himself . . . until a slow dance song came on! That was the end of his dancing until the end, when the deejay played "Sweet Home Alabama" and we all were celebrating and hugging and saying good night. It was a great evening. I am glad I went. I am glad T.B. asked me to do this. In return, I had helped him get out of his shell.

It began to be difficult to meet budget. The building payment was due each month. All the bills had to be paid monthly. Salaries had to be paid to staff. The reserves were being dipped into to meet budget, and we had tightened our belts all we could without breaking our backs. In the midst of this, there was a mission trip to Ukraine coming in July of 2004. We did an all-out chicken-que to raise funds for the trip. I was quietly steaming inside when the very ones who came to work wound up sitting around under the drive thru bad-mouthing the trip. Yes, they were Senior Adults. A few of them I was really disappointed with in their attitudes.

Nonetheless, the money was raised, and we flew to Ukraine for almost 10 days. I will detail this trip in a future chapter. God was working in me that trip. In the midst of loving Ukrainian people, God was breaking my heart and making me very uncomfortable. In my spirit I knew I was burned out, that I had carried the church as far as I could due to the "blue hairs" constant childish behavior in worship and other places. They were not about to allow any further change. They did not want people entering their fellowship lest they lose their power base. It was status quo or nothing. I knew in Ukraine that something had to change. It was breaking my heart. God had given me West Hall Middle School. On the train ride from Kharkov, Ukraine to Kiev I silently cried myself to sleep in that sleeper car for eight hours, knowing I had to deal with a decision when I returned home to Flowery Branch.

I returned exhausted. I was an emotional wreck. About a week after returning I was in Chuck's office just talking and sharing. I told him I was exhausted and felt that right now I was at a dead end in the ministry there at Flowery Branch. He shared with me how he was feeling the same way, and how two churches had contacted him with regard to pastoring their churches. I was taken aback. I then shared with him that four churches had been after me in the past year to join their staff and I had said no to all of them. Chuck leaned back in his chair. He said that in light of my being at a dead end and in light of the church's financial situation of really struggling to pay all of us and in light of God's urging me to do something, that perhaps it was time to consider a move to a new ministry. He then told me that Jerry Light had recently asked him if he, Chuck, would be angry with him if he approached me about joining the staff at Jodeco Baptist Church. Chuck asked, "Would you be willing to talk with Jerry?" I asked him how he felt about it. Chuck's ministry and feelings were important to me, too, not just my ministry. Chuck assured me that he would enjoy keeping me on staff, that I had done an excellent job, and that if I left he wanted to be sure I had a place to "land." I told Chuck to make the phone call and tell Jerry I would talk with him and the personnel team at Jodeco.

We tried desperately to keep this quiet so that the church remained on task and did not get sidetracked into talking and dividing over me leaving and speculating as to why I was leaving. Over time, though, it became obvious I was preparing to leave. People began to approach me and ask me. I told them the truth as gently and diplomatically as possible. I encouraged them to "hang on" and give the church a chance to get past my leaving and see what happens before they jump ship, because families began to tell me if I left, they were leaving also. I sincerely did not want that to happen to the precious people at 1st Baptist.

One by one, over the next two months, families began to be strangely absent from worship and Bible study. Every family was in the age bracket of 50 and under, with teenaged children or younger. At least six families over time left 1st Baptist Flowery Branch and joined other fellowships. That made me so very sad. During those days I often flashed back to the conversation I had with Jerome that if they insisted on changing worship styles backwards, they would lose everyone under 50. That had now proven to be prophetic. Jerome is a good and Godly man. Jerome has great wisdom and had given me excellent advice in the five years I served 1st Baptist. This was one time that Jerome was wrong. 1st Baptist's worship, as I understand it, is still struggling since my departure. The student ministry is a former skeleton of itself, with one parent there telling me in a recent conversation that they too were leaving because since my departure the student ministry was no longer a safe place for their 13 year old to attend. My heart was broken. Great things for God were destroyed by the selfish attitudes of a few who insisted on building a building, badgering us until worship changed, and throwing up roadblocks in our path to assure that no progress was made until their backwards and selfish demands were met.

I had to tell the students at the West Hall schools that I was leaving. I knew I could not do that until Jodeco had officially extended me the call to come and I had accepted. That time came. On a Wednesday, I shared with 1st Priority adult leadership that I was leaving. They were saddened, but God that very day had brought Eric Colson, a fellow student pastor, to that meeting to take up where I had left off. At lunch I began to say goodbye to the students at the Middle School. They were shocked and saddened and some were even angry that Wednesday. I told Travis and Caleb and Brian at their table what was happening. We talked and I thought we had said our goodbyes. It was painful for me, more than the students knew. I moved to another table to say my goodbyes there. A few minutes later, Travis and Brian came over to that table. Travis looked at me, took a deep breath, and then said, "Brian and Caleb and me were talking and tomorrow is our final football game that we will play at West Hall Middle School. We decided we are going to dedicate the game to you and win it for you as a going-away present." My heart was deeply moved by their love and compassion that they would do that. They were not even members of my student group.

A few minutes later, Dylan Bartlette came to the table where I was sitting. Dylan leaned over the table and asked, "Since I heard we are dedicating the game to you 'cause you are leaving us, Nick and I wanted to know if you would come to the field house and pray with us before the game?" I looked up finding it hard to choke back the emotion. "Dylan," I said, "I would be honored to do that. You be sure you get permission from Coach Newfall for me to pray with you, and I will be there. You or Nick just let me know tonight at ALIEN YOUTH what time I need to show up." Nick gave me all the information I needed. Coach Newfall gave permission and I was to show up at 4:00 to pray with them in the locker room. Thus, the football game that opened this book was played and all the years of loving students had come back to me in an amazing display of respect, love, and deep friendship.

I left that church knowing that I had been a more effective student pastor than ever before. God's hand was on me and I give Him glory for all the good things that happened. I also know that I left worship in great shape, and more powerful and excellent than it had ever been in that place. There are precious people in that church that I left behind: Larry and Becky, Phyllis, Bill and Laura, and others who were so encouraging right up until my last day at 1st Baptist. I know I left a legacy in Hall County that students all over the area are still benefiting from. May God bless 1st Baptist and bring her to be the church He always intended her to be.

CHAPTER FOURTEEN

A KID NAMED TRENT

His name is Trent Corey. Rarely in ministry does such a kid come along. I have had the honor and privilege to know him, mentor him, teach him, and love him and his family for almost seven years. It is a relationship that has transcended the student pastor/student role to become adult friend/young friend. He and his parents, brothers, grandmother, and niece have all become treasured friends whom I love deeply.

The kid who ran to me at the football game with the cell phone was Trent Corey. Why would I devote a complete chapter to one teenaged boy? As you read on, you will discover why Trent deserves a full chapter, for among teenagers I have met he stands out as an example of someone whom student pastor's dream of having in their student groups. He is that quiet teen who is seeking God and seeking to live as a clean, upright, Christian, well-balanced kid.

When Trent was only 10 years old he showed up one night with John Nation, Chuck's youngest son, for AWANA at 1st Baptist Flowery Branch. I loved him the moment I saw him. There was a quiet confidence about him that was rare for a 10 year-old boy. He began to attend regularly, and I began to uncover a very kind, tender, and loving spirit in him. He lived in John's neighborhood and was not attending church anywhere. Trent had already accepted Christ as his Savior about a year prior to attending church with John.

It was not long after he began coming that his parents, Deborah and Tom, began attending 1st Baptist because they saw the church loving Trent and having a positive influence on him. Trent was enjoying being a part of 1st Baptist. Soon, his parents were regular worshippers. Trent's grandmother was also attending with them, for she lived in the home with them.

One Sunday, Trent's father Tom came to the altar during the close of worship to talk with Pastor Chuck. Tom was a Christian but he felt he was now ready for baptism. Tom was baptized and Deborah and her mother, along with Trent's older brother, Matthew, joined the fellowship there. Trent continued to grow and develop as a young Christian through Sunday Bible study and AWANA.

He began to hang around me more and more as he moved toward sixth grade and the time he would enter the Student Ministry at 1st Baptist. I enjoyed being around him and discovered some interesting things about his life. Though he was only 11 or 12 he had already accomplished more than some do in a lifetime. I also discovered that he was easy to joke with. But, I also discovered along the way that if you pull a prank on him, he is probably going to strike back when you least expect it and in a way that is beyond imagination.

One Sunday after church, he was being my shadow and pestering me, still getting to know me. At this time he did not know me well enough to know how I will sometimes tease a person. I have a very subtle, sometimes cynical, and often strong sense of humor and often will tease people very hard. This particular Sunday morning Trent was picking at me and teasing with me while I was trying to talk to someone else. I decided to unload my big guns on him. I turned, stared at him, gently shoved him and then with a very loud and commanding voice I thundered at him, "You best leave me alone, punk! I have eaten sandwiches bigger than you!" Well, his eyes became as large as saucers. He looked like a deer in oncoming headlights. So, I looked at him, smiled and burst out laughing. He then knew he had been "had." The other kids standing around were laughing also because they knew me and my sense of humor at times. Once he got his sense about him, he made a great recovery. He grinned, poked me in the stomach and retorted, "Yes! I can see you have eaten a lot of sandwiches!" I began laughing. Here was a young boy that was sharp and witty and could hang with a master of teasing.

By the time Trent was in Middle School he had already achieved some tremendous things in his life. Trent is not one to brag about himself. He would never tell you the things I am going to tell you. He has a humble spirit that credits God quietly for all he has done with his life. He is amazing now. He was amazing then. Trent held the World's Record for his age and weight class in the Bench Press and Dead Lift for several years until a Hawaiian kid broke his record. He is a very gifted baseball player. He has played every position except first base and catcher.

Trent's first love in sports is wrestling. He has excelled and won many awards through the USA Wrestling organization. His Middle School and High School wrestling career is stellar. Through the years I have watched him become a master tactician on the matt. He wins time and time again. His sophomore year in High School saw him rise to the potential state champion in his weight class. Wrestling sick and with a broken nose for first place, at the very last second of the match, his opponent beat him by one point, which put Trent in fourth place in state. I consider that quite an accomplishment for a 15 year-old.

During my years at 1st Baptist I watched Trent grow up physically, and spiritually he took some great strides. When he was 13 he went on a mission trip to Montana with a team from 1st Baptist. He was permitted to go because his mom and dad were helping with the trip. His Brother Matt, now almost 16, went with us, also. Trent was one of those teens on the trip who just found things to do. He was active in the religious skits we did. His brother Matt played guitar with me and others who formed a praise band to play for some of the meetings we would do in Red Lodge, Montana.

Forever burned into my memory are two incidents in Red Lodge that Trent was directly involved in. There was an afternoon when we had decided to prayer walk the entire town, to walk and pray over Red Lodge. The little Baptist church on the corner was our launching point. As I left the church to begin my part of the walk, I saw Trent and John moving toward the skate park, a place where town skaters came to hone their skateboarding skills. I stood on the corner and watched. They walked to the fence, placed their hands on it, bowed their heads, and prayed for quite a while over that skate park. John was able to talk to one skater about Jesus later at that park. Trent's heart was to pray for the kids who use that park.

Each night we did a rally-type meeting for teens in the town. It consisted of the band leading in praise music, and the team doing skits, puppets, and sharing in a talk with the kids who showed up. Trent asked to speak at one of the evening rallies. I was floored. That evening I watched as this 13 year-old kid stood onstage in his sock feet with his Bible and shared his testimony and talked about how to have a relationship with God through Jesus. He did an astonishing job. I remember the lump in my throat watching him. Even at 13, God's hand was becoming more and more evident on him. He was "different" from other 13 year-olds. I have described him as being a wise old man in a kid's body. His quiet spirit, his level-headed way of thinking, his commitment to Christ and to high moral standards was becoming more and more noticeable.

From the wrestling and onset of puberty in middle school he entered his freshman year in high school. I had already shared with him that this new place in his life was going to be more difficult and challenging to live in as a Christian. I shared with him that he may have to make some hard decisions concerning his actions and his friends. Tony would put that to the test for Trent.

Tony Newman is a kid I have always loved. I got to know Tony because Trent began bringing him to church. Tony even made a profession of faith and was baptized. Tony is also a gifted athlete. I have personally witnessed him doing things on roller blades and a half-pipe that I never dreamed people could do. When Tony entered high school with Trent he began to change. He changed his image to a tougher look. He began to hang with some different people. His church attendance dropped off. Trent and I never gave up on him. We kept being his friend and encouraging him to come to church. He would show up occasionally.

One day when I showed up at the high school I discovered that there had been a drug bust there. Several of Trent's friends had been arrested and taken out of the school in handcuffs for drug dealing, drug use, and possession. Tony was one of them. I sat at the table with Trent in the cafeteria and we decided we would just pray for him. I know Trent cares for Tony a lot. So do I. I left Trent and went to Tony's home to see him. After a long conversation with his mother and prayer, I went downstairs to Tony's bedroom. He lay there under the covers sleeping. When I called his name he rolled over, saw me and reached up to hug me. Tony began crying. As we talked, Tony shared with me that the worst part of the incident was being led out of the school in front of his friends in handcuffs. They went through the whole trial ordeal and Tony did time in alternative school. He later had another incident with the law concerning drugs and as far as we know, he continues to use.

Trent was faced with the dilemma I told him about. There comes a time when you have to cut bait and run in some friendships. Trent had stood by Tony. He had prayed for Tony. Tony had even put pressure on Trent to try drugs. Trent continued to stand by him as a friend. Now, as of this writing, Trent spends as little time as possible with Tony. He understands that "if you hang out with pigs long enough you will eventually get some stink on you." Trent has made some hard choices about his friends. Jody, Tony, and others he used to pal around with are no longer his close friends because they have chosen a life of drugs. Trent now has friends who don't drink, smoke, or do drugs as far as he knows. He has made some tough but wise choices. He is an example of what can be for students when they have the courage to live right.

Trent has had to face difficulty in his own family. First, his oldest brother Bradley managed to party himself out of Georgia Tech, then he fathered a beautiful little girl out of wedlock and began living with the mother in a life of drugs and who knows what. Trent's parents are raising the child in a stable, Christian environment. In the midst of all that chaos, Matthew began changing his behavior.

The week before I left for the Ukraine, I found out that Matthew too had developed a drug problem at 16 and had become sexually active. During the mission trip I wrestled with how to approach him, confront him, and help him. He had become belligerent and borderline violent toward his parents. In that home too is the baby, talking all this in. Matthew had told his dad that he wished Tom and Deborah would just get a divorce. That way he would only have to deal with one of them. He had told them he wished they were dead. He threatened to kill them. Various forms of drug paraphernalia had been found in his room.

When I returned from Ukraine, Matthew was over at some friend's apartment. I drove over there, picked him up, took him to Oakwood Park and we sat face-to-face under the shelter where it was cooler. Unconditional love was about to be put to the test. I began by telling Matthew how much I loved him. I then told him what I had heard he was into and I asked him if it was true. It was all true.

In the course of conversation I asked him why he thought he had taken that path. He had to think about it. After a few minutes of clarification and leading him to think it through, he said, "It was a bad choice of friends, especially female friends." I then led him back to our mission trip to Montana, when he was bold for God and his heart was so kind and sensitive. Together we traced the journey of a young man who had let friends influence and change him over time into the person of the present. His blue eyes were cold and void as we talked. I began to question him about God. He knew he was away from God and even questioned some things about God. When I asked him when he thought he might be ready to come back to God, he said he was not ready right then. He paused, then he looked at me and said, "When . . . if I do come back to God, I want you there." I almost broke down and cried in front of him. I desperately wanted to reach across the table, tear his soul out, clean out the crud, put God in it and place his renewed soul back into his life. But I could not. I had taught Matt to play guitar. We had some awesome times in Montana together. We had eaten together. I sat there remembering the time I took Matthew to eat at an all-you-can-eat place. For dessert, he had mixed orange Jello with banana pudding. It was pretty disgusting to look at. But that was Matthew. All I could say to him was this promise, "When you are ready, if you will call me, no matter where I am I will come and be here when you are ready to come back to God. I promise you." I took his hand and then prayed for him as tears formed in the corners of my eyes. I am still waiting for that call.

Matthew had to move out. He wound up with his brother and his live-in. He has recently moved back home, shown signs of changing, but still stubborn, disobedient, and mouthing off. Trent had lived through all the stuff in the beginning of Matthew's addiction. I wanted to be sure that Trent was all right, not being neglected in the midst of everyone's focus on Matthew.

I made a date with Trent, picked him up and took him to Common Grounds Coffee House in Flowery Branch. We got our smoothies and went upstairs where we could talk alone. Trent was very upset with his brother. He could not believe the way he talked to their parents, the language he used, and the disrespect he showed. Trent has learned to hate drugs. He understood that Matthew being moved out of the house was to protect them and especially Cassie, his niece whom he loves deeply. The house had a sense of calm about it again now that Matthew was gone. Trent stood with his parents in the decision to get Matthew out of the house. Whatever his parents felt would help Matthew and the family too was fine with him.

Our conversation turned to him and where he was at growing up. He had no girlfriend. I knew the day would come, so I had a very frank, heart-to-heart talk with him concerning his relationships with girls. With guys, I am blunt. He got the message. I know he did. Some recent conversations concerning a current girlfriend confirmed that.

Trent is 16, almost 17 at this writing. He came and spent time with me recently. We climbed a local mountain together, sat at the top and talked for over an hour! I know he struggles with pressure from girls. He is a very handsome young man. Because of his commitment to weight lifting, wrestling, baseball, and to fitness in general, he has one of the most defined teen bodies you will find. But he assures me he has maintained his Christian convictions. I continue to monitor his life. His Junior year in school will be crucial for him.

Trent is not perfect. He's a boy. I'm sure he has not connected some things he does yet with the fact that Jesus probably would not do that. But in him I see promise. I see a teen boy trying to live as a Christian. I see some mistakes he is making here and there along the way. He learns quickly. My prayer is that Trent will never make decisions that are going to destroy him and short-circuit a life that is full of potential for God. I have invested a lot of my life in him and to this day I have a deep love and a respect for Trent and the life he is trying to live and for the man I see in him. May God grant you a Trent in your life, student pastor. It is in Trent and students like him that I understand in a fresh way that all students are not going to hell. There are some students out there quietly and powerfully living for God. Trent and students like him give me hope that the future is going to be safe.

CHAPTER FIFTEEN

STUDENTS AND MISSIONS

And so it was that I came to Jodeco Baptist Church. One of the great joys of my life has been to leave my comfort zone and go somewhere else for awhile on mission with a group of students. It is difficult work from the beginning, but the pay-off can be incredible when God really gets in the middle of the trip.

My first experience taking students on a mission trip came during my tenure at Second Avenue Baptist Church. I had a very talented, committed, and mature group of students at one point. They were beyond the normal summer retreat. I decided that it was time I launched out into the deep with them and do something to really challenge them. There were students like Harold Hilliard, Elisa Walker, Lori Bennett, Jim Kelly, and a host of other students poised and ready for me to raise the bar on them.

My searching for a project led me to Smoky Mountain Resort Ministries in Gatlinburg, Tennessee. Bill and Cindy Black have been resort missionaries at work in that area for years and have done incredible work. Only God knows how many lives have been touched for Christ as a result of their faithfulness. Several adults went up one winter weekend to look over the field, to meet Bill and Cindy, and to receive some help and instruction in how to begin to lay the groundwork back home. We included in that group one teenager, Dan Starnes. I wanted a student's perspective on the area and the work, a student involved in the planning from the beginning.

It was determined that we would do day camps each morning in six different campgrounds in the Gatlinburg area. That required six different teams with all their supplies and plans ready to go. Each evening the entire team would go to a campground and perform a Family Evening

Program for the campers there. The program would include music, dance, drama, comedy, and the gospel. This required a small portable stage, a portable sound system, costumes easily worn, and about 40 minutes of entertaining material.

And the rehearsals were on. The planning sessions for the teams began. These students grabbed the ball and ran with it and left for Gatlinburg extremely prepared for the trip . . . except for one thing. No one can know how many kids would show up for the day camps. No one could know if anyone would come to our evening shows. But we launched out trusting God, and God did not disappoint us. The day camps were running over with little kids daily. The students were falling in love with them.

They were selflessly pouring their lives out daily. At night, the evening programs were tremendous. These kids performed like professionals, and from their hearts.

I floated daily among the camp grounds to help with day camp. One morning when I arrived at a particular camp ground and approached the area where the day camp was being held I noticed frantic motion and work going on among the team and the kids. Then I spotted Heather Schwettman. She was always a very kind and sensitive person, quiet with red hair. As I approached she had this look of total exasperation on her face, then she began to cry. As I hugged her I asked her what the problem was. Here was the problem: so many kids had shown up for day camp that they had run out of the pre-cut bunny ears for the paper plate bunnies they were making. She was sad because not all the kids would be able to make a pink-eared bunny. I dove into their panic box to see what I could find. I found extra paper plates. I found markers. "Heather," I said, "these kids may not all have pink bunny ears but at least their bunny will have ears. We sat together and cut out more ears for the kids from the paper plates I found. If they wanted pink ears, they could color them with the pink markers we found in the panic box. Problem solved.

Did you see her heart? She was totally focused on the kids. She was not about to let them down. It is amazing what can happen in situations like that when a student pastor comes alongside a struggling teen and helps them get the job done. I have done that more than once. When we encourage them in such ways it builds their confidence. I saw Heather's tears turn into a big smile as the kids left happy with their paper plate bunnies.

Adam Turner is another kid that was on this trip. Adam was 14 with a brilliant mind, extreme talents, a killer sense of humor, and an attitude bigger than the mountains of Gatlinburg . . . at least at the beginning of the trip. During the course of that week as I watched Adam work with the kids in the campgrounds, perform in the evening programs, and interact with the other students during our afternoon "our time" periods, I watched him transform from a smart-mouthed kid with an attitude into a hard working maturing young man. His parents even remarked, wanting to know who the kid was I brought back and what I had done with Adam. My first mission trip . . . success.

I had the opportunity to travel with other student pastors to Connecticut on mission. We fanned out over the area and trained mission pastors in student work. I was assigned to Waterbury. I am a Southern boy. I was there in a northern town. People did not speak to one another on the streets. They would not even look at one another as they walked by. The buildings were dirty from years of exposure to industrial pollution. It was fall and that added to the gray mood of the area.

I found a group of people there in Waterbury hungry to know how to reach students. On Friday night I modeled a student worship meeting for them to attend and observe. A handful of students did show, enough for me to have a very good meeting for the leaders to observe. This meeting involved music. God showed once again he has a sense of humor. We flew in on Thursday night. Everyone's luggage came around the conveyor belt at the airport . . . except my very expensive 1973 Glen Campbell Special Edition Ovation guitar! My heart sank. I was feeling nauseous. I would do it all with keyboard and a cappella. I went to the claims office and filed a lost item claim. They began to track my guitar down.

I went home and stayed with the mission pastor and his wife that evening. I was so very disappointed that I would probably never see my guitar again. I had already mentally made plans to change the model meeting to run without guitar. Just a bit after 11:00 that evening, there was a knock at the door of their apartment. When the door was opened, there stood a courier holding what looked like my guitar! As I signed the paper I asked him where my guitar was all this time. He checked his paperwork, grinned, and said, "Your guitar has been to San Francisco and back today!" I thanked him, shut the door, and breathed a huge sigh of relief.

On Friday evening, the meeting went off well. On Saturday morning I met with those leaders who attended and observed what I had done. The idea was to have a round table discussion of questions and answers about what they had seen. And they did ask! These leaders were so passionate to reach students for Christ there. Some of the things they shared with me concerning teens in that area were heartbreaking. I poured myself out to them. I shared with them everything I knew in answer to their questions. The session even went longer than scheduled because of their desire to be equipped to reach teens.

A trip into Boston, the Harvard area, a meal and concert at the House of Blues, a Sunday worship with our assigned areas, and we were on the plane back home to Atlanta. It was my joy and honor to share whatever I knew that might help someone in a bleak town reach teens for Christ.

While at Tom's Creek, the Georgia Baptist Convention asked me to assist in putting together and going with a team of students to Jamaica on mission. JAMAICA FOR JESUS was the mission emphasis of the Convention in those days for teens. Dennis Rogers oversaw that facet of work. His invitation took me off-guard. I have always loved and respected Dennis Rogers as a man of integrity, honesty, and one who walks with God. I now had the chance to labor alongside him.

The first journey to Jamaica changed a lot of lives, mine included. This was my first mission experience outside the comforts of America. I saw a nation of people who are loving, warm, gracious, and hungry for the hope of Jesus. For two summers, Dennis and I traveled together to Jamaica with a hand-picked team of students who had applied for the mission, gotten letters of reference, and sacrificed a weekend to come to Perry, Georgia for an extensive interview with either Dennis, myself, or other student pastors such as Rick Smith. From there, the team was selected.

Then a phone call came one day that scared me, humbled me, and made me rise to a whole new level of leadership in my own life. Dennis, in his own quiet, loving way, had been mentoring me and training me. The phone call was from Dennis. The message was that he could not go to Jamaica that year due to other responsibilities with the Convention. He asked me to head up a team of students myself from the state and train them and lead them to Jamaica the coming summer. I was totally stunned. I questioned Dennis honestly. I did not feel I was qualified to do that. I asked him bluntly, "Do you really think I can do this?" His reassuring words came. He had trained me for two years. I had two trips under my belt. With the help of other student pastors such as Stan Green and Rick Smith I could gather, train, and launch a mission to Jamaica. And so I did.

During the ministry at Flowery Branch there rose an exceptional group of older students. I remember sitting in my office one morning eating a biscuit and drinking coffee as I read Scripture and prayed. I asked the Lord to show me a way to spiritually raise the bar for those teens. My eyes fell upon a souvenir from Jamaica there on the bookshelf. I picked up the phone and called Gordon Davidson at the GBC and asked him what mission opportunities were available in Jamaica for students the coming summer. The GBC was sending some teams down to the island. He told me that I could also bring my own team. He told me who the missionaries in Kingston were . . . Doug and Rebecca McHenry. I nearly passed out from excitement realizing that God was doing something special here. I attended college with Doug, a very smart, committed, and wise man of God now married with children and missionaries to Jamaica.

I contacted Doug and the process began. The students had to fill out an application, get letters of reference, and be interviewed by Yours Truly. Pastor Chuck also had to give his approval for each team member. I had set the age limit for this trip at 16 and older. God had other plans as we began the process.

There was a 14 year-old named Drew Perkins at 1st Baptist. I loved Drew for many reasons. For one, I have a soft spot for foster and adopted children. He and his two brothers were all adopted by their parents, Lana and Dennis. Drew was the oldest of the three boys. I loved Drew because of his spirit and strength and the way I saw him moving on from a past that was dark and abusive. His mother Lana approached me one day out of earshot of Drew. She shared with me how disappointed he was that he could not go to Jamaica because he was not old enough. It is all he had talked about at home . . . going to Jamaica. He had even cried in disappointment that he did not qualify to go due to his age. I questioned Lana a bit about Drew. I then found a time to talk with his father. Dennis shared the same things with me that Lana had shared concerning Drew's passion to go to Jamaica.

As I thought about all the dynamics involved . . . . Drew's past, his age, the maturity he was showing lately, the passion in his heart to do missions, the fact that he and his family each summer did a mission project, God spoke clearly to me that Drew was to be part of the team. I told his parents that my big concern was that Drew could possibly become homesick and it would be difficult for several reasons to send him home. So, if Drew would fill out the application, get his letters, and let me interview him I would put him on the team and I would put him in my room in Jamaica to monitor him closely as to his mood and security. They agreed.

Out of that team of Chase Ertzberger, Stacia Ertzberger, James Nation, Tiffany Davis, Drew Perkins, Doug Gladden, Chris Moore, and Keith Crandall, at least two of them are currently preparing themselves for ministry and/or missions. That trip was fun and it changed the lives of those students. A few anecdotes from that trip follow.

We were headquartered in Kingston, Jamaica in a quaint bed and breakfast inn that was totally ours for the week. It sat in the countryside hills just outside Kingston. We arrived on Friday. This was probably about three nights into the mission. Drew and I were beginning to settle in for the evening when I heard the girls next door screaming my name over this horrendous ruckus coming from their room. Drew and I sprinted into their room to find Stacia, Tiffany, and their chaperon Marilyn on top of the beds jumping up and down and from bed to bed screaming my name and the word "rat." I grabbed one of Tiffany's shoes to begin the mission to take out this vermin. She immediately left the room, came back into the room with one of my shoes, snatched her shoe out of my hand and put my shoe there in its place and said, "You are NOT killing that rat with my shoe!" We never found the rat. I discovered why he was there, though. The girls had a stash of snacks in the closet. We found a container to put their snacks in and seal off so the rats would stay away. We never saw the rat again.

Chase is a very special guy. He wrestles with Krohn's Disease. It's a malady that really has no cure and you spend a lot of time in the bathroom. Knowing this, Chase made the team anyway. One morning we all loaded up in our van driven by Ricky, a young Jamaican guy who had a wicked sense of humor and drove for a living on the island. I did the cursory headcount to be sure we all were present and accounted for. Chase was missing. No one knew where he was. I went back inside the B & B and began walking the halls and calling his name. As I turned to go down the hall toward my room I called Chase's name. From the community bathroom just to my left I heard, "FRRRAAANNNKKKKIIIIIEEEEEEEE!" It was Chase. I asked him if he was okay. Then he said, "Yes. I have sitting in here for 10 minutes trying to get someone's attention. I'm out of toilet paper!" I went down the hall to my bathroom, got a spare roll of toilet paper, set it by his bathroom door, told him I would meet him at the van, and went back to the van. Curiosity in the team pulled what had happened out of me. Chase came to the van and Ricky immediately dubbed him with the nickname "Chafe." In his Jamaican accent he then told Chase, "Mon!

Here in Jamaica when there is no paper we just use our hand." Then he immediately held out his hand inviting Chase or "Chafe" to shake his hand. The van exploded with laughter as Chase quickly declined the handshake. That nickname still haunts Chase today.

Chris Moore. What a dude! Chris was a jock, a wrestler with a very gentle and loving spirit. The Jamaican kids who came to the day camp each morning were attracted to Chris for those reasons. He was a kid magnet. I heard this uproar one morning as I rounded the school building we were using to see this huge pile of Jamaican kids on the ground in a huge cloud of dust. At first glance it appeared a riot had broken out. Chris' mom, Marilyn came out of the building to view this mountain of arms and legs and giggling and laughter. I waded into the middle of them to begin to bring some order back. When I got to the bottom of the pile there was Chris, dirty and laughing, loving every minute of the attack.

Doug approached teaching the teen-aged kids that came with fear and trembling. This really got Doug out of his comfort zone. But the kids that came loved him, he loved them, and he did an excellent job of practicing "flexibility" with those students. There were two teen boys who came, one named Fabian. They caddied at Constant Springs Golf Course just a block away. In talking about golf I told them I did not play golf because it was quite a frustrating game. They asked permission to leave for about 10 minutes. I granted it. When they returned, they had with them a five-iron and their pockets full of golf balls. During break time, the three of us went to a clearing behind the school because they were determined to help me play golf. By the end of that session with those two boys, who showed me how to stand, grip, and swing the club I had gone from barely moving the ball three feet to rocketing the ball way over the fence into the adjoining neighborhood. As successful as their lesson was, golf is not on my list of sports.

Drew. I had allowed him to be on the team with fear and trembling. Drew turned out to be the hardest working and most sensitive person on the team. Not once did I ever sense homesickness creeping in. He became the kid who saw something that needed to be done and just did it without having to be told or even asking. He was the person on the team that God put there to minister to the "one." Drew could often be seen sitting under a tree with one kid that no one else would play with or that was having trouble socializing with the other children. He was the person on the team who stopped the three year-old from toddling out the door by picking them up and loving on them. Drew understood in his own way the loneliness and lack of stability and love in the lives of those children. While he was there, in a beautiful way he showed those precious Jamaican ghetto children the love and warmth Jesus can bring to their lives.

Drew also took on the role of our team mascot. The older boys loved on him and encouraged him so much. One of the funniest things I witnessed on this my last trip to Jamaica was Drew stuffed into his long gym bag with the zipper all the way up to his neck. All you could see was Drew's head poking out the bag as the other boys carried him around the bed and breakfast.

The following year I took another group of teens and adults to Red Lodge, Montana. John and Joy Monroe faithfully serve God in a very difficult, humanistic arena. Red Lodge is a tourist town. It is very quaint and lovely. In the winter skiing on the mountain is king. We came one July to help reach some of the teens in that town. We did different things to help during the day. We might go to the public pool and swim with the kids and build relationships with them and invite them to our evening rallies. Some of the kids like John and Trent would go to the skate park and hang out with the skaters. One morning we went door to door in practically the whole town handing out flyers and inviting people to church.

But God has a way of stretching mission teams. One of the first things I teach a team is that they must stay flexible and be ready for anything to change that is planned once we get there. I had not planned a time for church clean-up on this trip to Montana. When we arrived and started looking at the building and the grounds, there was great need for cleaning, straightening, window washing, and yard work. Some of the men and ladies on the team went to a store and bought a weed eater and flowers. One man borrowed the next-door neighbor's lawn mower. Inside, some of the women tackled the kitchen, cleaning it up and organizing it. Out in the sanctuary, some of the teen girls and guys were dusting and straightening chairs. John tackled the windows with spray and towels inside and outside the church. Flowers were planted outside. The lawn was mowed. The walkway was edged. The weeds were trimmed. It was looking great! And what did I do?

I did what no one else wanted to tackle. With a brush and cleaner, I spent the morning scrubbing toilets for Jesus. With my head in those toilets I prayed for the church. As I polished the fixtures to a spotless shine I asked God to prosper John and Joy. Yes, you can even scrub toilets for Jesus if that is what He has in mind for you to do. With every scrub and wipe I was praying over that town, that church, the missionaries and their girls.

Each evening we did what amounted to a student worship service complete with drama, music, puppets, and testimonies. One evening Josh, who lived in my home, did a powerful presentation by dragging a huge cross down the aisle, sharing a powerful talk, and then using the cross for us to nail our sins to as a reminder that in Jesus our sins were nailed to the cross. The praise band consisted of Derek Dunagan, John Nation, Matthew Corey, Randy Searcy, and me. We led in praise and worship music each night. The pastor's wife, Susan, led the puppet team each evening in some skits. Other students did live drama, some very funny, some with a powerful punch. Some shared their testimony. Trent, Josh, and Randy were among those who spoke. During the course of the week we saw several teens come to Christ. Of the students who went on this trip, four are preparing themselves for ministry.

Summer of 2004 was incredible. I was part of a team from 1st Baptist Flowery Branch and a sister church who went to Izyum, Ukraine for a 10 day mission. The plan was to run a day camp at the church each morning, run soccer camps during the afternoon in partnership with the Baptist church in Izyum during the day followed by evangelistic meetings at the church each evening. God took our plans and bent them to his own. Flexibility played a huge role on that trip.

First, in Ukraine, girls do not play soccer. It is strictly a boy's sport. More boys showed up for soccer camp each afternoon than we anticipated. We had to roll with that. Each afternoon tons of boys from 7 to early 20's would come to compete and hone their skills in soccer. Soccer is huge in Ukraine. We were allowed to use two fields at two schools in the city. Both were relatively close to the church, one within walking distance. While games were being played and other teams were waiting their turn to play the team pulled out all the stops for those on the sidelines.

Susan ran puppet skits. I would pull the guitar out of the case and immediately have a dozen children around me. Brian would use the Evangicube and have boys standing around him listening through an interpreter. Pastor Chuck would speak at times. Often I would be one-on-one with a boy wanting to talk. The interpreters worked hard in the afternoons! Sometimes I would be throwing a ball with a small group of boys. I remember that one boy wanted to learn how to throw an American football. We happened to have one in our bag of tricks. I spent 30 minutes showing him how to throw a spiral and then throwing with him as others gathered to join the game.

There were so many boys I could write about. I will share a few with you. There was a group of soccer players who were the typical teenage macho jocks. The group was made up of Andray, Dyma, Anton, Kolya, and Anton the goalie. These five boys managed to steal my heart. The first time I saw them they sat on the hill next to the fence at the soccer field changing clothes and jockeying with one another. Kolya suddenly approached me that first day and shook my hand. Then he handed me a box of matches and in broken English welcomed me to Ukraine and through motions told me the box of matches was a gift from them. I thanked him, waved to the boys, and went on about my business.

I sat down and pulled the guitar out of the case, adjusted the tuning, played a bit and just waited. Here they came with others. Anton the goalie was really tough. He smoked and was very cocky. I sat there wondering what song I knew in English they might be able to relate to on some level. "Every Move I Make" came to mind. It has a whole section that is only "la, la, la, la, la, la, la!" Through my interpreter I told them when we get to that part that they could sing it. And sing it they did! The whole neighborhood rang with the "la, las" those guys were booming out. I had them right where I wanted them. Through the interpreter I told them the message of that song. These five guys became my body guards. I guess they just sensed the love of Jesus in me to them somehow.

Susan, who was Pastor Chuck's wife, and I shared the same burden for that group of boys and agreed to pray for them to be saved. A few days later at soccer camp, Anton came to me wanting to talk. He knew enough English taught him at school that he and I could communicate without an interpreter. Here was a strapping 17 year-old boy in a country who had only been free about 10 years. We sat on two tires half buried in the ground on the playground right by the soccer field. Anton wanted to know why I came all the way to Ukraine from America to play soccer with them. I shared with him that I chose to fly thousands of miles at my own expense because I wanted to share God's love with them, and soccer was the means to do that. He only knew Russian Orthodox religion. I must sadly report that the Russian Orthodox Church is a very dead faith. It is all ritual and tradition and really had no meaning for Anton. I shared with him how God showed his love for us by sending Jesus to die on the cross. I simply encouraged him to think about that and consider giving his life to following Jesus, not religion.

Ukrainian people are very intelligent and well-educated, some of the smartest people I have ever known. They enjoy conversation and talking about ideas. They will not commit to anything until they have thought about it and know the cost. They approach Christianity the same way. They TOTALLY commit. Anton was thinking about what I shared. I continued to pray that Anton and the others too would come to Jesus.

Meanwhile, Anton the goalie was hurt, could not play, and that opened the door for Susan to share Jesus with him one afternoon. Anton the goalie prayed and received Christ. How do I know he was serious? Ukrainian people do not commit until they are ready to totally commit. Also, the next day you could see the change in his life. There were no cigarettes, and his attitude had gone from cocky to strong leader among the boys. God had changed his life. There was still Andray, Dyma, and Kolya.

The final day of soccer camp came. My boys were all there. Following the championship games the teams, coaches, and referees were to walk to the church for a soccer rally to give out rewards, hear the band made up of Derek Dunagan, John Nation, Susan, and me, and to hear the gospel. That late afternoon the church began to fill up with boys as Derek, John, and I quickly sound-checked and tuned. Extra chairs were brought out. When they stopped coming, over 200 boys packed that church to the hilt, the largest crowd ever to assemble in that church. Pastor Lonya was beaming. The band played. We did "Every Move I Make" and the boys in the back were up in the chairs booming out the "la, la" portion of the song. The place was rocking!

Every soccer player there received new soccer socks that we brought from America. The champions were recognized and rewarded with soccer jerseys and other awards. Then Pastor Chuck took the microphone with his interpreter at his side at a second microphone. Chuck simply preached the love of Jesus, the plan of salvation. He then called for commitment from them. 58 boys stood boldly and professed Jesus as their Savior that night. Among those boys were Andray, Dyma, and Kolya. I was overwhelmed with joy in the Lord. My soul was full! I sat down by Losha, one of the church kids there, and wept openly with thanks and praise to God. My boys were saved. God had heard our prayers and honored our efforts. We hugged all around that night. The boys made a beeline for me beaming with the love of Jesus on their faces. The following day the team would leave for home. The boys told me in broken English that they would have a present for me when they came tomorrow to say good-bye.

The next day we met at the church with bags packed for the drive to Kharkov, the train ride to Kiev, and then the flights home. Here came the guys up the street finally, as we were saying good bye to the church people there and getting organized to leave in vehicles. They presented me with a piece of paper. On one side was a certificate printed in Russian. In the blanks were written, "Frenkie Wiley for the best friend Ukraine youth." On the other side Kolya had drawn a picture of the four of them with me in the middle. It is in color, and it captures the "look" of all of us. Across the top of the picture is written "Ukraine love you!" I hugged every one of them. I had gifts for them too-Snicker bars. For Americans a Snickers bar is no big deal. There, they are something teens usually will not buy for themselves. I also made sure they all had Bibles and that they would be faithful to be baptized with the time came and stay in church. I then said goodbye to a group of the church teens. And it was time to go. I remember time almost going into slow motion, like in a movie, as I walked to my car and the boys walked down the street shouting, "Goodbye, Freeeenkie" The backs of their heads eventually faded into the others on the street. Five soccer players in the city of Izyum, Ukraine had come to a new life in Christ. It all began with a box of matches.

There is one other teenaged boy I want you to meet. His name is Losha. He is representative of all the boys and girls in that church, especially Volva and Arturum. This group of teenagers knows what being a servant is about. Losha's looks draw you to him immediately. He was 15, a bit small for his age, slender, with blonde hair and ice-blue eyes. He was a quiet kid with a humble spirit. I am not sure what drew him to me. I would enter the church, sit down in the mornings, and he would find his way over to sit next to me. He became my personal roadie. When we went to some high- rise ghettos there to put on programs to draw kids and witness to others, Losha went with us. He carried my guitar for me there, got it out of the case, and then put it back when I was finished. He did the same thing in the afternoons going to and from soccer camps. I came to love this boy deeply for his Christ-like spirit and his servant's heart. We never talked much. There was an unspoken bond that developed between Losha and me. It seemed enough to him that he was just near me.

He and the other teens in that church were great help to us. I came to love them all. Losha became that very special person to me that God is preparing to use mightily I believe. The evening when all the soccer players were coming and professing Christ, Losha was right there watching me as I cried tears of joy. I saw tears in the corners of his eyes, also.

On the street the morning of our goodbyes, I called all the church guys together for a time of good-bye. Through my interpreter I told them how very much I loved them. I thanked them for all their help with the sound system and carrying things. They had even gotten involved with the puppets! To express my love for them I gave gifts to them. I have Arturum and Volva Snickers bars and guitar picks. They both could play and sing beautifully. I gave Losha a Snickers bar and a pen. I hugged them all good-bye. I was okay until I came finally to Losha. As we hugged, we both lingered and both cried together. Losha put my bag in the car that would carry me to Kharkov. His servant heart was real and good. I pray even now that God uses Losha, Volva, Arturum, Andray, Dyma, Anton, Kolya, and Anton the goalie along with other Christians in their generation to bring a great nation, the nation of Ukraine to the day where she truly is a Christian nation.

Student pastors, take your students on mission trips and even local projects as often as you can. The impact on their lives will be incredible. Teenagers are at a stage in life when they are the center of the universe. It is all about THEM. Mission trips and projects do several things for students. It gets them away from their comfort zones. It gets their eyes off themselves and gets them focused on others. When they begin to see that others have needs, their hearts open up and beautiful things start happening. I have witnessed students grow spiritually more in one week of mission work than in a whole year of teaching, or in a week at the beach on a retreat. It also opens their hearts for God to speak. I think of students I have been honored to be pastor to down through the years that are either in ministry or are preparing for ministry. Ben Hansard, Bobby Newman, Matt Evans, Tiffany Davis, Derek Dunagan, Jeffrey Davis, Chris Moore, Billy Roberts, Steven Johnson, and Alan Bradley all heard the voice of God to them in mission situations calling them out to serve Him vocationally.

The preparation and execution of a mission project, especially one overseas is fraught with all kinds of challenges and hurdles and difficulty. Remember, God is able. The end result of a difficult mission trip makes it all worth it. The one word I live by in planning mission trips is "flexibility." You make good plans. Prepare well. Be ready for anything God might do, because once you are on the mission field your plans are going to get changed. You may have to cut bunny ears out of paper plates. You may have to scrub toilets for Jesus. You may end up going places and doing some things you had not planned to reach a foreign country for Christ. But you will always see God's guiding hand moving you when you approach mission work prepared. Notice I did not use the word "planned."

In my years of ministry there is at least one thing I have learned-prepare, but do not plan. That may sound strange to you. Yes, you should study and prayerfully get ready for any ministry you are going to do. But God's work is a lot like surfing. I recently was in Florida and watched some young guys surfing. They pulled into the parking lot with their boards strapped to the roof of their cars, or protruding from a rear window. They had on their board shorts; they covered themselves in sunscreen, strapped their boards to their ankles and waded out into the water. Those boys were prepared for surfing. They paddled out into the deeper water, turned toward the shore, and lay there on their stomachs looking over their shoulders waiting for the perfect wave to ride as far as it would take them. Those boys could not plan the waves, but they rode whatever the ocean sent them!

Ministry is the same thing. You prepare for ministry. You get your tools ready. You pray and study. You love the people. You are always looking over your shoulder waiting for the wave of ministry God is going to send you. When it comes you minister just as much as you can on that wave. Then you wait for another! You cannot plan ministry any more than a surfer can plan the waves he rides. You can be prepared and in the right place with the right tools seeking God for the wave He is going to send and then ride that wave of ministry with all your heart. You never know. Jamaican kids, people on vacation in a campground or a mountain resort, or a bunch of soccer players in Eastern Europe may come to the Savior. Every wave of missions and ministry I have ridden has been different . . . unique. Each wave has been full of His glory and blessing. The sooner you can expose students to this, the better the future of ministry and the church, the body of Christ is going to be.

CHAPTER SIXTEEN

SOME THINGS I KNOW

I have learned some things in 33 years of being a Student Pastor. There will be more I learn in the years ahead. With each generation of students new challenges, needs, and attitudes arise that call for fresh approaches to ministering to students. I have seen Student Ministry go from "spiritual babysitting" to an army of Godly men and women who are committed to meeting the deep needs of students.

I have seen the problems and needs of students grow consistently worse with each new wave of kids. Early in ministry I dealt with name calling, the ups and downs of dating couples, some rudeness to authorities, and the occasional fight between two boys. As divorce rates increased, as mothers began giving birth to children addicted to or affected by the alcohol or drugs the mother used, as moral standards plunged year after year, as more and more women gave birth to children and remained a single mom, the devastation on their children I have seen the problems become exponentially deeper and more serious.

In just the past year I have ministered to students in the throes of drug abuse. I have helped three young girls who were sexually abused by the same college student, two of them at a church camp two years ago. I have seen students formerly in student groups I pastored turn to homosexuality. And a new twist . . . I am seeing parents more "screwed up" than their kids. They are rude. They spread lies. They cause trouble in churches. Even when their kid is wrong he's right. There was Joey. It was common knowledge among the students in that church he was doing drugs. He had also told me that he had been experimenting. The truth was that wild parties were going on at his home on weekends and drugs and alcohol flowed freely. Joey had told me that, too. The whole student group knew what was going on. One Wednesday evening after student worship as kids were filing out Joey's mom came storming in demanding to talk with me. Her mood was so intense I knew that the lingering kids had no business hearing what was about to come out of her mouth. I moved her to the back area where we did counseling for new Christians. I sat down in a chair and before I could even ask her how I could help her, the flood of anger and hatred spewed forth from her mouth.

She proceeded to tell me that I was not fit to be a student pastor. She loudly proclaimed that she would have my job. She then accused me of breaking a confidence that Joey had placed in me and now all the kids knew he had a drug problem. I sat there and took it. I knew I had said nothing that was not common knowledge and let her know that in no uncertain terms. She seemed shocked and diffused! I told her further that it was common knowledge among the kids before Joey had ever told me he had a problem. She had no comeback except "what are you going to do about it?" I told her I intended to love Joey and help him any way he and she would let me." As she walked out of the room I was rather proud of myself because I knew another piece of information that I could tell no one, but almost threw back in her face. Thank God I held my tongue and like Mary, pondered this in my heart the rest of my tenure at that church. The information I had was powerful but I chose not to use it: It was she who was supplying the drugs and alcohol for the parties.

The depth of issues with students today from bulimia, cutting, homosexuality, and divided families, kids with no father in the home either physically or emotionally, and the continuing battles with alcohol and drugs and immoral dress, especially among the young ladies calls for us to get all the training we can to deal effectively with the fallout. It demands that we stay before God for our kids like never before. You need to stay fresh in God's Word daily seeking insights into Scripture and how the principles embedded there can be practically applied to the needs of your students. It is essential that we get involved in their culture. That means visiting the schools regularly as much as you are allowed. It entails you spending some money to go to football games and hang out with students there. You need to show up at the local "hangout" whether it's a mall or a parking lot unexpectedly and watch students. You may see your own there. They need to know you and you need to know them beyond the walls of the church. They need to see us as valuable adult friends who understand and are comfortable in their world. You need to meet and build relationships with as many of their friends as possible. It enlarges your ministry and gives you greater insight into the students you minister to. When you step in front of your group to teach you will have ammunition from those experiences that will increase your effectiveness in reaching those students.

There is another group of people you MUST get to know-the parents. That is a challenge today. You may well have to get to know step-parents as well as parents on both sides of the student's family. Earlier I mentioned Elgin's family. There was his father, his step-mother, his mother and her husband. There was also his step-mother's former husband and his wife. There were six adults who were parents on some level to Elgin. I almost never sorted it all out. You minister to whole families when you are a Student Pastor. The impact you have on their child's life impacts that family. If bridges are built to parents in the process, when disaster strikes a home, you can have an open door of ministering to that family and possibly reaching those for Christ who may not be Christians. Your families will also be much more willing to volunteer their time and effort and money to student retreats and other events if you have taken the time to build those relationships with them.

There are several ways to do this. Visit them in their home. If a child of theirs is in the band or on the football or basketball team, sit with them during the games and cheer your lungs out for their kid, your student. Take time to speak to them about home life. For example, I lived in an area densely populated with Delta Airlines employees. Delta was having a difficult time financially. I just asked those families in my church occasionally about that . . . quietly, discreetly, but sincerely. Seeing this coming, one of the reasons I led the church to pay the accompanists is that one of my accompanists has a husband who works for Delta. They have three wonderful kids. That was a quiet way to minister to them in love, and help them at the same time. Another thing you can do is get in their kids' corner when trouble is afoot in their lives. When they know you love their kids and have their best interest at heart, you have the parents.

One of the things in ministry I have had to do from time to time is to milk rattlesnakes. Now I do not come from a snake-handling background nor would I serve in a church that had a box of death in the front of the worship center and invited people come stick their hand in there and pull a serpent out and play with it. I think I understand now what that last chapter in the book of Mark that deals with taking up serpents and not being harmed is really getting at. To my colleagues deep into theology I apologize if I am out of bounds theologically here, but this is my take on that part of Scripture, and it has nothing to do with literally picking up a rattlesnake or a cobra and daring the Holy Ghost to let it bite you.

Trust me; there are rattlesnakes in your congregation. They are in every church in America. Some of them are deacons. Some are Sunday School teachers. They are on Personnel Committees, in the choir, the nursery. Occasionally they have blue hair. Sometimes they are teenagers. Their rattlers shake out dissatisfaction, anger, gossip, lies, and vitriol. Most pastors hate Monday mornings. That is when the rattlesnakes in their churches slither to the church office to complain about the music, a certain teacher, something someone said, or how bad the finances are, or to subtly threaten the life of the pastor or staff in that church if things don't change. Rattle! Rattle! Rattle! Rattlesnakes will also crawl on down the hall to the Student Pastor's office to hiss about the rowdiness of the students, the way the girls dress and what you are going to do about it, and that awful noise called music that emanates from the student center on Wednesdays. Rattle! Rattle! Rattle!

When the griping and complaining reaches a certain level, if you don't "drain the venom" you can get into trouble. Sometimes you have to just milk a few rattlesnakes. If you do not and they have rattled long enough, they will strike. They will financially boycott you. They will remain seated during praise and worship when everyone else is standing trying to worship. They will grab a kid in the hall who has a skateboard and slam them against the wall and threaten them if they ever see them in there again. Those strikes kill the spirit of a church.

How do you drain the venom? When a rattlesnake side winds into your office and starts hissing, LISTEN. Do not react. Let them rattle as loudly as they want, Let them vent. When they have completely exhausted themselves and all that venom has been drained out of them, then you can respond. Sometimes, your best response is no response. You thank them for sharing. At times you have to let them know firmly and lovingly where you stand and that you are not moving. Remember those deacons at Tom's Creek? There will be times when you must walk them through to the end result of what they are demanding. They have probably not thought that far ahead. They just want something done. Remember Jerome. There will also be times when you can change some things to make a situation more tenable. Bring them onboard, if possible, to help change the situation. Sometimes you just have to milk some rattlesnakes.

Student Pastor, you must also guard your own life and integrity. I have seen and heard the horror stories of Student Pastors crashing and burning. I am a bachelor. Several of us bachelor youth guys in one city had an unofficial club we belonged to, the BTR Club. The BTR stood for Bachelor 'Till the Rapture. I will be a bachelor until the rapture. Most of those great men of God have gone on to marry and raise families. Awesome for them! Because I am single I have not had to balance time between church and family. Most Student Pastors will marry. When they do, they find that there is a constant battle for time between spouse and kids, and church and that student group. DO NOT neglect your family. They come first. One of the finest examples you can be as a married Student Pastor is one of a loving father committed to his children and his wife. Our students need that kind of role model. I do not want to see Student Pastors building great ministries but at the end of the day realize they have totally neglected so much about their own families.

You also need some time for yourself away from that church, the office, the rattlesnakes, and even your family. As a single minister solitude is easy to find. One pastor-friend of mine told me that I have solitude down better than anyone he knows. Not so for the married minister. I have to make time for solitude. I consciously put myself in places weekly so that God can speak to me because I am away from the phone, the TV, the computer, the church, and those rattlesnakes. You need times of refreshment. I find that being on the beach alone on vacation really refreshes me. That is where I write new praise music. Take some time to refresh your own soul. Your spouse, your children, and your church and those wonderful students will thank you for it!

Guard yourself morally. I have some rules of thumb I follow that have helped me down through the years as I have instituted them into my life. I NEVER am alone with a female in a car, especially a student. If a female comes to my office to talk, if my office door does not have a large window on it, that door is open during the conversation. If you have teenagers in your home, be sure another adult is present with you. I never eat alone with a woman in a restaurant if a lunch or dinner meeting is necessary. Do not give any ground for the rattlesnakes to begin rattling and strike. Too many Student Pastors have fallen by the wayside due to moral failure in this area. Good men and women of God have had to step down because of moral failure. Watch where you go on the computer, Student Pastor. No one should ever have any reason to search your office or home computer for indecent pictures.

Be careful how you deal with money in your church too. It scares me to death as a Student Pastor because no matter how organized I get, when students are signing up for a conference or retreat they will just walk up to me and hand me money and tell me to sign them up. I have a system. Right in front of the kid I fold the money or check and put it in the top corner of my wallet. That is how I identify money handed to me that is not mine. I keep meticulous records on computer of everything handed to me. If it is cash I label it as such. If it is a check I even put the check number in the computer file. When I turn in monies to the secretary I go over every bit of it with her. She has a record of what I have a record of so it all comes out even. We always have a paper trail. Financial indiscretion can be just as deadly as sexual sin. Never put yourself in a position where anyone can question you about church money. If they do question you, have your documentation there so they can clearly see how the money was handled. Be above reproach in your dealings with what people perceive is God's money. Their perception is correct.

Another thing I know is that you must keep the lines of communication with your pastor open. I have been blessed to serve with some great men of God. From Lester Buice, Richard Lee, Lamar Barden, Ken Ross, Haywood Day, Clack Stubbs, David Matthews, Chuck Nation, to Jerry Light, these are all unique men of God that I have joyfully served with. One of the regrets of my ministry is that in my earlier years I did not take the time to really get to know some of these men on a more personal level. With some, it was a strictly professional relationship. Richard Lee was like that. In the two years I served with him I only saw him "let his guard down" once. It was difficult to get to know him personally. He is a great man of God. I was probably intimidated by him somewhat, being new to the ministry at the time. I have always wanted to know him more outside the pulpit and those great books he writes. Rev. Buice on the other hand was like a grandfather to me. Here I was fresh out of seminary. He took me under his wing and loved me. He was always so kind and forgiving of my blunders. Clack Stubbs taught me how to really stand for what I believe. Chuck Nation and I share a common love of music that drew us together as good friends. Take time to get to know your pastor. How you relate to them will have an impact on the effectiveness of your ministry. I have even served with a pastor younger than I am.

Even though I was older than my pastor, as a courtesy to him I always put a copy of the worship service planned for the week for him to look at. He needs to know what his worship leader is doing. In Student Ministry, the pastor needs to know what you are doing and often WHY you are doing it. At one church I did an "IT HIT THE FAN" NIGHT where we had a huge commercial fan set up outside facing a covered wall on the church building and we just threw stuff into the fan to see what would happen. Flour, sardines, ketchup, sugar, a huge bag of croutons, and other gross things found their way to the wall through the fan. At one point a student even stood at the wall and took some of the things we did. If you are going to do something like that, you had better have a good theological and spiritual explanation of why you are doing such a thing.

Another thing I know is this. If you are going to catch fish you have to have the right bait. My dad was an avid fisherman. He had keys to every pond in Turner County in South Georgia. He knew what to use to catch fish and even when to use it. He taught me to use top water plugs early in the morning, and go deep later in the day. I learned that catfish like bloody things like liver. Other species of fish will eat a cricket. Some like worms. Fish would tremble at the sound of Dad's Ford Ranger pulling into their pond area down there!

You and I as Student Pastors are fishermen. We are after "catching" some kids for the kingdom. Now, if you are going to catch students you have to use the right bait. And this is where so many church members just do not "get" student ministry. I have learned a line to use when someone complains about methods I use to reach students. When a well-meaning church member says to me, "I don't like that screaming music those kids had at that meeting the other night" I will smile and respond with this- "I don't like worms either, but fish do." When they start in on you with complaints about that lock-in that they did not like, smile and say, "I don't like worms either, but fish do." You don't draw students to hear the gospel and have the net drawn by having The Cathedrals in for a youth concert. WRONG BAIT! Now, The Cathedrals are fine I am sure. Southern Gospel is not the bait for students. They are not going to "bite." Bring in a group such as Casting Crowns, Third Day, or a Christian hard-core band and a school of students the size of Texas will show up and you can share the gospel with them. I personally do not allow any screamo music. I only allow hard-core if the lyrics are understandable. The grunting, growling, guttural vocals do not lend themselves to understanding words. I have affectionately called this "puke" singing. The point is that you must use the right bait to reach the kids. If I were reaching senior adults I would use southern gospel and Bill Gaither-style music, but I am out to get kids into the Kingdom of God. I would never sponsor a lock-in at a go-kart place for our senior adults. They would have me fired. Sponsor the same event for students and you will have more teens on the ground than you can imagine. Be sure you use the right bait, even if it may be something that you personally do not care for.

Another dynamic of your ministry as a Student Pastor is this. Have you considered your responsibility to the pastor's teen kids? Reality is that pastor's kids often have a difficult time in a church. You as their Student Pastor can be helpful in making their teen years in church positive and loving and meaningful and smooth. Here is what often happens with PK's.

PK's understand intuitively that they are considered "different" by most people. They are watched more closely than other teens in the church. The expectations seem higher for PK's than other students. They sense that pressure while inside they just want to be like the other teens in the church. How you deal with your PK's can help them experience "just being a member of the group." Allow them to find their own level and area of service just as you do the other students. When John Nation became my drummer in Flowery Branch I really did try to let him find his own level of commitment that he was ready for. There were times I had to protect him from members of the congregation when it came to those drums. I can say that John was faithful without me "putting the screws to him" to play because he was not only talented but was also the preacher's kid and I expected him to do it. I allowed him to serve as he was ready and in the manner he wished to serve.

Sometimes you will need to go to bat for the preacher's kid. You will need to stand in the gap for them and be their advocate. I have seen church members who get bent out of shape with the pastor. Instead of going to him, they become passive-aggressive and take shots instead at his family. I applaud the pastor's wife who takes so much dung from people at times. When church members can't get to the pastor's wife they WILL stoop low enough to say unkind things to their kids and even do unkind things. I remember a day in one church where the pastor's son was a skater. He was practically joined at the hip with his skateboard. The only thing I had asked the skaters not to do was to skate inside the building and to stay off the front steps and railings of the church. They pretty well obeyed me. One day the pastor's son lost his mind, forgot, or was testing the rules as he was prone to do at times. He was skating in the downstairs hallway. A man in the church who had a "beef" with his dad grabbed him around the neck, slammed him against the wall, and threatened him verbally about what he would do if he caught him skating in the building again. The boy was 14 and yes, he should not have been skating in the building. That was not the issue for the man involved. For him the issue was, "I don't like your dad so I am going to take it out on you. Here is my chance." Let it be known that the pastor was not at all happy about what that man did to his son. Neither was I. We put the man on notice that if we saw him ever put a hand on ANY kid at the church again, that he would be explaining it to the police very quickly.

Pastor's kids are just like any other kid. They need a safe environment where they can learn about God and experience His love through the people there. Unfortunately, they often come to understand that church people can be some of the meanest people on earth. I have seen a few PK's graduate High School, leave home, and turn their backs on the church never to return because they want no part of people who claim to be headed for heaven but act as mean as hell itself. You may be the only one, Student Pastor, who makes the difference for those teen preacher's kids who come into your student group.

And finally, I want to encourage Student Pastors to learn the ministry of Kleenex! Teens' hearts are broken easily. The combination of first love and hormones is a recipe for disaster and hurt. When couples break up and the tears flow, often the best thing you can do is keep your mouth shut and just hand them a Kleenex and offer a hug. You will see girls often crying for what seems to you as no apparent reason. Give them a Kleenex and a hug. A boy has probably broken their heart. I have even seen big, strapping 260 lb. football players break down and cry. All hail the power of women! That football player may just need a hug and a Kleenex. About the hug . . . you may want to ask him first. Teen males can be very homophobic and look at ANY guy who hugs them as suspect. Besides, that boy could probably hurt you! My point is, an act is often more powerful than tons of words.

Down through the years I have been called upon to go to high schools to help counsel students in times of grief and disaster in those schools. Tony Kendall died in a diabetic coma in Tucker. There was Joe's death in Toccoa.

West Hall High School lost Jenny Melton. Luella High School recently lost Sarah Edwards. In the funny, happy, care-free world of teenagers, the ugly side of life intrudes suddenly without warning. At West Hall High School I hugged necks and passed out Kleenex to tons of emotionally distraught teenaged girls. Yes, I even hugged 260 lb. linebackers on the football team. They entered the cafeteria one by one crying and broken. I hugged those guys and handed them Kleenex. I sat with them. If they talked I would talk and respond to their questions and queries of "why?" If I sat in silence, that was okay too. They knew I was there for them. I did not have to say I cared. My very presence and the simple act of a Kleenex said it for me. At Luella, the students walked to the accident site where Sarah's life here ended. I saw many girls and guys from the Middle School there who had recently attended the lock-in Jodeco had sponsored. What was my role amid that sea of students? I patted kids on the back as their emotions started to crumble. One 13 year old boy standing next to me kept holding it, almost breaking, sniveling, choking it back and trying not to cry. I finally could not stand it any longer. I whipped a Kleenex out of my pocket handed it to him and then just patted him on the back gently in a side hug. He let his emotions go. He needed to. I handed a girl who had been to the lock-in a Kleenex there at the crash site. She looked at me through tears and said, "Thank you . . . OH! You are the guy from the lock-in. Thank you."

Student Pastors, show compassion to students who need it. Guard your life. If you are a married minister, your family comes first, NOT your ministry. Build good relationships with your pastor, and help guard his kids from the onslaught of those in your church who would use his kids . . . and yours as a whipping post for the pastor or you. Milk some rattlesnakes. When you drain the venom in so many church members you really are diffusing things that could bite you later if you do not take care of it now.

My prayer for your ministry is that you be powerfully successful in building God's Kingdom. We are in a time where the temptations and hurts and questions students have are deeper than ever. It is up to you and me to show them by our lives and our ministries that unconditional love of God. They have to know that there is love in the world that has no strings attached to it. They need to know that there is a place, the living church of Jesus Christ, where they can find unconditional love. I pray that your ministry to students will be that place.

CHAPTER SEVENTEEN

INTO THE FUTURE . . .

It is a warm Thursday afternoon in early September at the football stadium. It is a year since that emotionally charged day at West Hall High School. It is two different football teams. It is a different town, a different county. Earlier in the week I walked with many of those students to the crash site where a high school student died on her way to another day as a student at Luella High School.

I came to Jodeco Baptist Church in October of 2004. Jodeco Baptist Church is a church full of potential and promise. It is the most racially diverse congregation I have ever had the privilege to serve. On any given Sunday morning as I looked out over the people gathered for worship I would see white people, Japanese, Cuban, African American, people from Guyana, mixed race people, East Indian, and Hispanic. Racially, it looks more like the church ought to look.

Jodeco is also the most dysfunctional church I have ever served. I have never seen one congregation with so much drama. It seemed that every family had some issue or drama going on. This makes it very challenging to minister to the needs of the people. My personal opinion is that many of these people who profess Christianity are not Christians. I say this based on their behavior toward one another, their immaturity, and their "it's all about me" attitudes.

Jodeco is almost 20 years old, still a very young church, barely out of her teen years. Like young adults, Jodeco Baptist is in the process of trying to understand who she will be in the body of Christ, her real purpose for being. In 20 short years these wonderful people have endured wave after wave of spiritual attack from the enemy. The focus of attack has been mostly in the areas of worship and student ministry. Leaders have gone almost as quickly as they were hired. Personality quirks, inexperience, lack of training, and questionable morality have been the demise of past leaders in both areas. In the process, the church has grown weary and even cynical toward leadership from the pastor right on down.

I am old enough and I think wise enough now to understand that if the enemy can shut worship down, disrupt the student ministry which impacts whole families in the process, and demoralize a church, the power of God will not be tapped into the life of that church as it could be. The church will be so busy handling crises that it cannot focus on worship and on reaching the community for Christ. Thus, all this drama existed there.

That uncertainty was fueled by two people. It is amazing that as few as one or two people with agendas can quench the work of the Holy Spirit in a congregation. This year and a half has been challenging. It came to light that these people were behind the demise of the previous pastoral leadership. During the interview process one of them began to second-guess me during a Q & A session with the congregation before I was even called by the congregation to join the staff. While on staff, I was second-guessed as to a special effect in the Easter drama. I was told only part of a conversation so that it would appear that the pastor had lied to me. I was challenged as to the date of the Christmas Dinner Theater. With words taken out of context in an article I wrote to the students in their newsletter I was accused of using my position to politicize and create controversy among the teens. In each situation when the truth came to light, I was vindicated. Their power base was beginning to crumble.

I spent much time during those days, broken-hearted and weeping before the Lord in the quiet of that auditorium at the close of many Mondays. I found it hard to love these people. It was only through prayer that God gave me wisdom each time the accuser came and allowed me to continue loving these people. As mean as the attacks on me were, they were even more spiteful toward the pastor. I saw the damage inflicted on him, his sweet wife, and three precious children. I began to consider leaving.

I had seen in less than a year the choir rise back to strong levels of attendance, with the potential to explode as the church began to grasp that she must reach people, not do events. Student ministry was growing. The summer Breakaway was spiritually powerful and transforming for the large group that attended. The power wannabe's could not abide any success or event not done by them. So, in one final assault, they showed their true colors in a business meeting by creating controversy over the budget and attacking one more time the integrity of the staff. Choir, Student ministry, and the other ministries suffered at the hands of these in this final attack. But, the rest of the membership finally opened their eyes. They saw what had been going on for years and decided enough was enough. Their power base crumbled around them. They quietly resigned all their positions and exited Jodeco.

After that exodus, people came out of the woodwork offering to get involved in ministries like never before. The Men's Ministry took off like a rocket. The Angel Food Ministry began growing swiftly with orders now double what they were. The Student Ministry reached a major goal of establishing a student praise band and moving to a student-led weekly worship especially for teens. New students were slowly showing up and there was renewed interest and excitement among the students. The worship choir has increased in membership. There was a growing concern now that Jodeco really start reaching out and winning the community to Christ. There was harmony again in the fellowship.

For almost two years Jodeco was without a pastor when their wonderful first and only pastor Ralph Wade retired. The church did some very creative things during that time. They divided into teams to handle the ordinances of the church, the various ministries of the church, the care and maintenance of the church buildings and property, and events.

There is that word again . . . "events." The thinking of Jodeco has been that by doing big events people will come and be on the property, then maybe start coming to church there. The flaw is that the church has not received that return in the numbers of people, especially in the number of dollars spent on big events.

There was the annual July 4th Celebration. Jodeco is blessed with millions of dollars worth of property, over 40 acres, some of it wooded and still pasture land. It is perfect for fireworks. Each year for three years Jodeco sponsored an afternoon and evening of musical entertainment on an outdoor stage especially built for the event. Door prizes were given away during the evening. There were tents for children's activities and food as well as a product area where people could purchase CD's and other things performers brought with them. The conclusion of the evening was a tremendous fireworks display that is absolutely the classiest fireworks display I had ever seen. Traffic stopped on nearby Interstate 75 as people could see it from there! A thousand people or more turned out each year on the grounds of Jodeco for the event.

So, what is the issue? There has been no evangelistic outreach to those people while we have them on the grounds. We get their names on cards as they register at the gate, but there has been little to no follow-up. Pastor and I raised the bar to accomplish that that. The event team ordered bottled water with our own Jodeco label on it. It had our ministry schedule and phone numbers and the website address on the label. Jodeco church members intentionally would go to a tent where those bottles were kept that night, get some of the bottles, and go into the crowd offering cold water to people for free. People were trained in advance to open up a conversation with them with the view to find out where people were spiritually and to invite them to Jodeco. The registration cards were sorted through and un-churched people were culled out for visitation. I can tell you that my student Sunday Bible teachers followed up on cards with students for their classes.

The teenagers at Jodeco are some of the most gifted, loving, sensitive, people I have had the pleasure to minister to. They are talented. There are several very good guitarists among them. Many of the students sing well. They have a flair for acting and do well at dramas and skits. They sincerely struggle with having an honest walk with God. They were very much like sheep without a shepherd, waiting for someone to show them the way to go, to love them, be firm with them, give them clear guidelines, and be a true Godly influence on them. For some reason, God had sent me to be just that and it scared me to death daily.

These students are awesome. However, when I first came, several of the girls, from middle school to college aged, did not know how to dress modestly as Christian young ladies. They came to church showing tummies, with their jeans slung down to there, and their tops up to there at times. I very quietly put out the word around the church and among the students that my expectations were for them to dress as Christians.

After about three months of quietly and at times with humor, reminding them to be more modest in their dress, the stomachs began to be covered up and the wonderful young ladies in the group began to dress much more modestly. It was such a change that several of the senior adults mentioned to me that they had noticed a good change in the girls' dress around the church since I had come.

In April of 2004 I took the cream of the crop to DARE2SHARE. This overnight conference is intense! Greg Stier and his staff do an incredible job of grabbing the hearts of teens right up front, and then motivating and training them to reach people for Christ. Not only does he do that. He works in a food drive during the weekend for students to go door-to-door to gather canned goods for a local shelter and have opportunities to actually put into practice what they were trained to do a few hours earlier. This conference rocked my students to their core.

On Friday night of the conference, Greg had all the student pastors stand out in the aisles near their student group. He challenged the students to go to their student pastors and tell him who God had put on their hearts to share Christ with back home. One-by-one they came. Crying and broken the students whispered in my ear the names of people God had spoken to them about. Finally, one of my 13 year-olds moved out. His name is Kyle. He was completely broken. For a while I just held him and hugged him because he was so emotional. I finally looked into his tearful blue eyes and asked him who God had put on his heart. He could not say. He did not know. I simply asked him to keep listening to God over the weekend and He would eventually know and that by taking the step Kyle had taken God was going to honor that. Some of my students remained in their seats, but they too were praying and crying and definitely wrestling with their own decisions. Kyle later came to me at the place where we stayed the night and told me he knew that God wanted him to reach his cousin Brandon. I hugged his neck and we prayed together briefly.

A few weeks later in our *24/7* weekly student worship on Wednesday, Brandon showed up with Kyle. In that meeting I simply ended the talk with a brief sharing of how to be saved. Brandon responded and was saved. God honored Kyle's faithfulness. Kyle and all of us were crying. Brandon was hugged and welcomed into the family of God. This was only the beginning of what would become a sustained revival among our students and God saving people. It was happening so fast! Four months into ministry at Jodeco and the student group was catching fire.

Worship was fragmented. It was like a TV show when I arrived. There would be a song, and then a pause for a commercial message! Then maybe another song or the children's message would be done, then perhaps another "commercial." It was clear to the pastor and to me that we had to take possession of worship. Everyone was using worship as a time to promote their ministry, their activity, or their event, an infomercial sprinkled with songs, Scripture, and a message. I immediately began to teach my choir and instrumentalists what worship really is. There was a need for them to see themselves in a new light. They are worship leaders too! We are a team! The focus during worship has to be on GOD, not us and our agendas. To that end we have moved worship to the point where the musicians understand more clearly their role, and announcements have stopped. If you do not watch the video screen before worship and read the announcements in the bulletin each Sunday, you are in trouble. There are now no verbal announcements from the platform before, during, or after worship. The people are given a greeting from the pastor from the platform, the choir marches in and we get our worship on without interruption. Worship began to flow smoothly now. It became more meaningful. I noticed a marked change in the spiritual atmosphere when we began this format. Worship became absolutely electric some Sunday's. When the accusers left, the altar would pack out on Sundays at time. One Sunday, I saw people quietly move across an aisle and just put an arm around someone and pray for them right there. There was a fresh wind of the Spirit blowing at Jodeco.

One Sunday, God really showed up in power. Pastor had a very challenging baptism to perform. The person had AIDS. He had made peace with God and desired to be baptized. After baptism this man returned to the sanctuary and sat by his mother. Worship progressed and there was an awesome presence of God. The choir stood to sing "God Is Still Doing Great Things," a solo with choir from Brooklyn Tabernacle. That song resonated with power and anointing as the soloist and choir sang. There were several in the choir becoming emotional as we sang. I had no idea what was going on in the sanctuary behind me. After worship, one of the ladies told me what was going on. The man with AIDS leaned on his mother's shoulder during the song. At first, they thought he was tired and even sleeping. Then they began to see it. The man was quietly weeping as the choir sang hope into his life. I am glad I could not see that. There is no way I could have gone on without totally breaking down emotionally. God moved powerfully in worship.

It never fails. When God is going to send revival to a church He usually uses a group of young people. Some of the greatest revivals in history began with teenagers. After DARE2SHARE, our students began to gather at the altar during the invitation time of worship to pray. Sometimes they prayed for each other or one in particular if they knew things were tough for them at the time. They prayed for their church. I noticed that adults had begun to gather with them for prayer at that time.

DARE2SHARE was only the beginning. In June 37 people went down to Panama City Beach for a retreat that I had planned and prepared and prayed over to be an intensely spiritual experience for them. I called Brad Beasley and his wife, friends of mine that I knew had an anointed ministry of worship and music for kids, and he brought his band down for the week. I brought an experienced Bible teacher from Jodeco who was young and knows how to communicate with High School students effectively. My favorite group to teach is Middle School kids. I love them, and I taught their Bible group. It was a week of intense Bible study, quiet times, loads of fun things to do too, and intensely powerful worship each evening led by Brad and Christy.

God swept the place all week! The discipline problems were really ZERO, nothing outside the little minor, normal teenaged stuff. The kids were well-behaved. Monday night worship was intense. Tuesday night was awesome. On Wednesday night, God blew us all away. I had asked the students on Monday to come to me and tell me if they would like to give a testimony of God's power in their life in the Wednesday worship. Three students were lined up, Heather, Jamie, and Billy, all older students.

That night, the band cranked up and the worship was super charged with the power of God. Students began weeping, lifting hands, and even praying for one another in the middle of the music. I knew God was up to something. As the band played I sat at a table quietly and asked God what I should do as it was obvious He was really moving and it seemed He was changing the direction of my talk. As I prayed I felt a hand on my shoulder. I continued, not looking. When I finished praying, there was Kristen, one of my precious young ladies in the group, who had laid her hand on my back and was praying for me. That still means so much to me that she was sensitive to my struggle and came to pray with me. After all that, it was time for the students to share.

Heather came to the microphone first. We were stunned and moved to tears and we all wept loudly as she shared a painful and difficult story of how she was date-raped one night and how God had used her close friend Christine to help her work through all of it. To this day I consider Heather one of the most courageous young women I know. Jamie shared a story of confusion and wandering for a time and how God led her back. It was awesome. Then Billy stepped to the front. I loved Billy. What a tremendous young man! Tradition in his family dictates that he will go to college, but not just ANY college. It had to be Georgia Tech. Plans had been made. He had been accepted to Tech. All he had to do was show up to move in and start class. He shared how even at DARE2SHARE God had been dealing with him. It had never gone away. God was once again dealing with him about becoming a youth pastor. He stood in front of the group and surrendered to that in front of them that night. Again the tears flowed and applause broke out.

Then it was my turn. I stood in front of the group almost too full to talk without weeping. I simply shared how we need each other, how God has given us each other as precious gifts. I talked about unity and staying unified. I shared how Jesus is a friend that is closer than even a brother and how to be saved. That night, Kyle's other cousin stepped out and received Jesus as his Savior. Kyle had not stopped with Brandon. Brandon was at this retreat too, but Kyle had now moved on to another cousin who needed Jesus. God had honored Kyle's commitment. In three days God had galvanized the group. On Thursday night, four more stepped forward to be saved. To God be the glory! Great things He has done! The church back home stood up and had to take notice of the radical change in the students God had done.

Then August came and it was time for the students to return to school. I always like to plan a huge event to celebrate back-to-school and to draw the net for souls. I challenged the students to have 100 people in the building for the Mega Lock-In. I had rented out a place where we would transport the kids to where they could bowl, ride go karts, use the batting cages, play laser tag, and shoot pool all night long. That night 120 people were present for the lock-in. The students did an incredible job of packing the place out. Kyle, yes . . . there he is again, had half the 8th grade football team from Luella Middle School that he played on there, as well as many of the cheerleaders! The evening began with NEWBORN FREEDOM in concert. They had the students from the first note. They gathered right in front of the band and there was "pogo-ing" and crowd surfing and singing during the show. There were also hands raised and worship from the kids as Eric and his band led the students into worship before I spoke. I had not really "planned" a talk. When I saw who was in the building I knew exactly what God wanted me to do. Many of the guys on that football team were also on a baseball team with Kyle. I had been to their games and watched them. I shared the plan of salvation as a baseball game. First base is admitting you are a sinful person. Second base is believing that Jesus is who he says he is. Third base is receiving Jesus as your Lord and Savior and walking His way. Then you get to go home! I had spoken to large crowds before with less passion, but that night I felt God's hand on me so heavily that I shared with passion and conviction and love. When the altar call was over, 20 students stood with tears in their eyes receiving Christ, many of them were Kyle's friends he brought to a lock-in and to Jesus in the process. God was all over the students at Jodeco.

It had been a year since arriving at Jodeco. I simply tried to build relationships with the people, adult and teen, and find ways to show them God's love. I quietly prayed for some changes and fasted on behalf of this church. There were some spiritual strongholds in the fellowship that stifled the life out of the body. God is faithful. Conversations between the pastor and me turned more and more to what God was doing in changing the hearts of those precious people called Jodeco.

God was doing some awesome things for these students. I baptized a 15 year old named Luke. Luke was an incredible young man. Luke was Cuban and had a younger brother James. Luke was a very bright teen. It just takes some time for a thought get from his brain and out of his mouth. When he first came, he would not even talk. He finally began to talk freely. Both James and Luke, when they first started coming to church, could not wait to leave. They were always bugging their mom to leave quickly after each service. Now you have to run them out the door! Lauren and Kristen were the older sisters of Kyle. These girls emerged as leaders, with deeply sensitive spirits and a concern that we reach people for Jesus. There is Lauren and Alex, my preacher's kids. These two girls are so awesome. Alex was keenly tuned with the attitudes of people, and armed with a sense of humor just as sharp. Lauren was the thinker, the more serious one, but had a funny side also. Lauren was a huge bundle of potential for the Lord. Jennifer and Kathryn are sisters. Jennifer plays guitar in the praise band. She is one of the most deeply caring and mature teens I have met in some time. She deserves a whole chapter alone. Kathryn is also beginning to step out as a great leader for Christ.

Steven was a unique young man. Jodeco has seen his family through more than one difficult experience, from living in a car, to an ugly divorce that broke Steven's heart, to his father's re-marriage. Steven had a strong faith. He sensed God calling him to ministry. He was a very good singer, with a voice that had potential to be even better than it is.

Josh and Brittany were brother and sister. Josh was a tough case at home. He did not even want to come to the Wednesday 24/7 worship for teens. He finally began coming. Each week he walked in the door, signed in at the table, grabbed a chair, pulled it against the wall away from the seating area, and just sat. The students began to gently "tease" him into sitting with them until he finally began sitting on the front row and actively participating in the worship and studies.

Blake was my drummer. Blake was the typical off-the-wall musician/drummer. He had this sick sense of humor that kept me scratching my head. He improved every week in rehearsals with the band to the point that I finally put him in front of the student group on Wednesdays with full drum set instead of just the Djambe. Curtis was my cowboy/redneck guitar player. He was really good with a guitar. He grew in his faith after a period of struggle. I came to really love Curtis. My bassist was Chuck, an adult who had graciously given his time to play with a bunch of teens. His bass lines have pulled the band together and really tightened them.

The icing on the cake was Michael, my last of three guitar players in the band. He came to us out of nowhere. He showed up one week at 24/7. He brought his guitar the next week and wanted to play with the band. He did play and did it well. I invited him to rehearsal. He came and I put him doing specialty parts on the guitar to sweeten the sound and add depth and variety. He fit in really well, a God-send. I came to love Michael more and more each week. He exhibited a servant heart and a growing faith.

There are other students I could share with you. It seemed since the parting of the accusers there was a new spirit and things were moving fast. A couple joined the fellowship. They played instruments. I planned to include them in worship and create a worship ensemble that would maybe grow into an orchestra.

But, on July 2, 2006 I officially retired from Student Ministry. The stress and strain of dealing with combination ministries as worship leader and student pastor got too much for me to bear. I felt tired all the time. This gave me a much-needed "out" of Jodeco Baptist Church. I was never totally happy there. After a very successful mission trip to St. Lucia, I made the decision to retire. I retired from student ministry and resigned my position there effective immediately, having no place to go. I did not fully understand why Jodeco turned out the way it did, but I trusted that God had a plan. And Boy! Did He have a plan!

CHAPTER EIGHTEEN

FINGERPRINTS

I moved back to Flowery Branch and the Corey's graciously provided me with a job and a place to stay. I worked in a company that builds exhibits for major corporations to show off their products at trade shows. It was manual labor in a warehouse pulling wall frame parts as orders came in and we prepared an exhibit for shipment to the trade show venue. It got me back into shape. God used those months to shave 35 pounds off my body. I got into really good shape working there.

Not only did I get into good shape, God reminded me of some things that I had perhaps forgotten. There is a world of people out there just struggling every day to survive, make ends meet, and take care of their families. There were men and women in that place from all over the world. There were some very "earthy" individuals there whose language would peel paint off walls. Some were going through divorce. Some were struggling with their kids. Others were struggling with their faith and would talk with me about it. Some were very confused about this faith they saw I had.

I knew I had to be very careful about the way I lived, especially around them. It would have been easy to pick up the profanity and use it because I was constantly bombarded with it there. I can honestly say that no matter how I felt, no matter how frustrated I was, no matter how harshly my boss talked to me, I never once resorted to profanity. I can honestly say that I lived my faith in front of those men and women while I was there. I only pray I planted good seed that will grow into salvation for those there who did not know Christ.

Those five or six months are a blur. I rose at 4:00 a.m. in order to be at the plant between 5:30 and 6:00 a.m. I would get home at 3:00 or 4:00 p.m. exhausted, shower, get a bite to eat, check e mails, watch a little television and have a quiet time with my Lord, then back to bed by 9:00 p.m. only to do it all over again Monday through Friday.

I did find a great church in Hopewell Baptist Church in Gainesville, Georgia. The worship music was incredible and so refreshing to my spirit each Sunday. I eventually joined the choir. The preaching of Pastor Robbie fed me and helped me begin to heal up from the hurt I had experienced at Jodeco. I came to understand that I was actually beaten up emotionally for a year and a half while there. Hopewell and her people were a source of healing for me.

After five or six months in Flowery Branch, I decided to move home. Churches were not beating my door down to hire me. I did not want to wear my welcome out with the Corey's. In December of 2006 I moved into my parents' home. I applied and trained as a substitute teacher. I began substitute teaching as I waited to see what God was going to do in my life.

My first morning on the way to the High School to teach, I passed by a church sign. When I read the name of the pastor on the sign I nearly wrecked my car I was so shocked. It read "Rev. Rodney Brown, Pastor." Rodney's father was my childhood pastor growing up. Clint Brown led me to Jesus at home and baptized me at Sycamore Baptist Church. That meant that Rodney and I were childhood friends for years. He was at my house or I was at his house practically every Sunday after church and any other time we could hang out together. We were the pre-teen and teen terrors of the community. Rodney is two years older than I am.

One morning I had gone to the county library to use a computer. Guess who was the county librarian? Rodney's wife! On this particular day as I was leaving the library, in walked Rodney to take his wife to lunch. We stood in the foyer and talked. Being a preacher's kid he knew what it was like to get beaten up by a church. His church, Trinity, had been through some tough times. It seemed that she was about to die. We promised each other that we would stay in touch.

It was not long until my phone rang and it was Rodney. He was to be away one Sunday and asked me to fill the pulpit for him. He knows my family and he knows me. He knows that we stand for Jesus Christ. He knows that I really seek to daily live for Jesus, especially now. I preached both sermons that Sunday for him. He received rave "reviews" from his congregation when he returned. It is interesting to note that there were maybe 20 in attendance the Sunday morning I preached.

It was not long after that when, one day as I was again leaving the library; Rodney's wife chased me down in the parking lot. She shared with me that Rodney had been meaning to call me and ask me to play piano for a revival at the church. I called Rodney and the deal was done. That revival was like old times. I played the piano. Mr. Charles Hardy, a wonderful man I deeply admire and respect, directed the music. He had been Sycamore Baptist Church's music director when I was a kid playing piano there. Charles Underwood was the evangelist, a former pastor of Sycamore Baptist Church. Each night, attendance grew. There was a tremendous spirit each service. I do not remember what night of revival it was, but several of the members "accosted" me to come and be their worship leader. They had no pianist or director. Rodney had been leading the congregational singing to CD accompaniments of hymns. On the final evening, I told Rodney that I wanted us to pray about me leading worship there. I knew they could not pay me but I was willing to come and play piano as a volunteer to help him and to help the church. After all, Rodney is a true friend. I returned Sunday to play piano. I walked in the front door and Rodney "hollered" me into his office. He sat down with me and told me point blank that the job was mine. He wanted me to take all the music and to lead worship, moving the congregation toward a blend of contemporary worship and traditional hymns. That day I began. Since that revival, God has been moving people to Trinity left and right. In five months the church grew from 18-20 in worship to as many as 86. New classes have been formed for Sunday Bible study. A women's ministry and a men's ministry has begun successfully. Worship has been God-anointed and powerful. A praise team was launched consisting of five singers, guitar, piano, and bass. The next part of the plan, God willing, is to grow a choir from that which will back up the praise team.

There was a huge surprise for me one Sunday evening in business meeting from the church and from my pastor. Rodney brought up how God was blessing the worship and the attendance and the church finances, and asked them to consider paying me for my services. He tossed out one figure and the church raised it! It was not much for a month, but I was so grateful to them. For a church that size what they had decided to do was very sacrificial. Now I had more income, too. At this writing, God is continuing to bless as each week the church is seeing people come to Christ or move their memberships.

I had been substituting for teachers since moving home. I have been toying with the idea of becoming a certified teacher. I basically have to pass the GACE in my field and do a year teaching under a mentor. My Aunt Sandra teaches at a middle school in a nearby county. She called me up one day out of the blue with an offer. Mr. Robinson, the choral director there, had been battling cancer and would be out for six weeks for follow-up radiation therapy at a hospital in Florida. He and his wife would live there in a facility for cancer patients receiving daily treatment as he would be receiving, and only be home weekends, effectively knocking him out of teaching for six weeks. She asked if I would be interested in the job. She had him call me. A meeting was arranged with him, the high school choral director, and the county school arts person. We discovered he was also a graduate of the Shorter College music program! After questioning me about my musical background, education, and experience, they referred me to the principal. We met briefly and talked. I then went to the Board of Education office and filled out all the paperwork, went through the fingerprinting and FBI background check, and filling out MORE paperwork, and I got the job. In fact, they have told me since, they had no idea who they would have asked because there was no one they know who could take a chorus class and actually keep it on track and not just baby sit a class as most subs do. I taught, I mean TAUGHT, those 7th and 8th graders each day. We worked rhythm exercises, did sight-singing, gave exams, worked on vocabulary words, and got the music memorized for the Fall Concert.

I had the privilege to direct the Fall Concert. There I was onstage with over 100 middle school students who sang their hearts out. At this writing, I may go back into class for a few days though my term has run out. He is still having some health issues that do not allow him to return to class.

In all this, we discovered that my dad had chronic leukemia. Treatments began with oral chemotherapy. That seemed to be slowly working to help him. A month ago, they tried a stronger infusion-type chemotherapy that he violently reacted to and it nearly took his life. My mother and I watched him quickly deteriorate from there. On October 15th, my father died. God is merciful. He had reached the point where it was difficult for my mother and me to take care of him. Dad could not leave the house during his final days. His remark one evening said it all. He said that he felt like he was in jail. I was teaching when he died. I left the school to meet my family at the hospital. The days following are a blur. Friends and family constantly flooded our home with food, love, prayers, and just being there. My church has been awesome. Rodney led the music at dad's service. Mother's church has been incredible, too. Bro. Ray, their pastor, did a great job at the service. I am going to miss him. The whole county is going to miss him.

I noticed Tuesday morning on the white door of the hall bathroom some fingerprints. As I looked at them it was obvious that those prints belonged to my father. Fingerprints . . . I guess his prints are all over the house. He took good care of it for almost 50 years. I have thought more about his fingerprints. His prints are also all over his church. He loved his church, Sycamore Baptist Church. As a deacon he saw to it that the church was guided safely through rough waters when they came. He also knew the physical plant there inside out. He was on the House and Grounds Committee. He would tell me recently from time to time where a pipe, or a joist, or something in the church was. His prints are all over that church.

His fingerprints are also all over the people in this county. Time and again, people would say that you never heard anything bad on Mr. Charles. I never did, and he was my dad. His prints on the life of a man who is a recovered alcoholic. My father helped him when no one else would. Now, the man is saved, sober, and loves being in God's house. At the funeral, and in our home during the days leading up the service, black people came to see us. My father coon hunted with a man named Lonnie before he ever married my mother. Every Christmas dad would load up tons of stuff and play Santa Claus to him and his kids and grandkids. Lonnie eventually came to Christ. Those nights in the truck listening to the dogs run were opportunities of witness that dad did not pass up.

A black man name Nicky came. Dad worked his father in the hardware store he managed for years. Dad then started Nicky in the repair business. Nicky has never forgotten that. Dad was practicing a love for all kinds of people when it was not so popular. His fingerprints are still on that man's life. One pastor at the service strongly emphasized that dad could enter any home in the county, be they black, white, or brown, and be welcome.

But dad's fingerprints are also on my mother, my sister, and on me. He lived before us the kind of life that made you proud to be his child or wife. He walked his talk. He lived what he believed. He instilled in us the value of hard work, love of family, respect for all people of all color, and even respect for animals. He taught us how to look beyond ourselves and meet the needs of others. We were not rich by any stretch of the imagination. Dad always helped those who had less than we were blessed with. I believe God honored that. We always had plenty. We had the good things of life like love of family and friends, and love and respect for the Savior God. The good things were enough.

Though he fished and hunted, he would not catch or kill anything that was not going on someone's table. He loved nature. My mother, my sister, and I all have great respect for nature and we all have unique ways of expressing our love for God's creation.

Dad was practicing unconditional love in front of everyone he met. He let the love of Christ show through him. Jesus loved everyone unconditionally. My dad was just simple enough to believe that if it was good enough for Jesus, it was good enough for him. His legacy is huge, much larger than I imagined. He was an example to me of unconditional love. I guess I got it from him. His fingerprints are all over me.

I have determined in my heart before God as a result of all I have come to understand about dad, that I will pick up his mantle from this day forward and seek to continue his legacy. I will continue to be a man of my word. If I tell you I will do something I will. If I will not do it I will tell you that, also. I will look more closely at others around me. If there is a need I can meet, I will seek to meet it. I will walk with God and serve God with new integrity, so that from this day forward, no one can say a discouraging word about me. I will continue to love people unconditionally. I will not judge them. I will let God do that. I will seek to love them and help them and show them God's love through Jesus Christ. After all, Jesus loves me. He has never judged me. He loved me so much that he died in my place, forgave my sin, and helped me live a life in touch with God. I have not lived a perfect life. No one has. But God has been gracious and merciful to me. Already in my life in the past 34 years, looking back I see my dad's influence of helping and loving others being lived through me. God has picked me up time and again when I would fall down. God's love is unconditional. Whosoever will may come to Him, no matter how bad you think you are and no matter what you may have done. God loves you unconditionally. Have you accepted His unconditional love?

www.ingramcontent.com/pod-product-compliance
Ingram Content Group UK Ltd.
Pitfield, Milton Keynes, MK11 3LW, UK
UKHW041953230426
12048UKWH00008B/308